JOURNE
GERMAN I

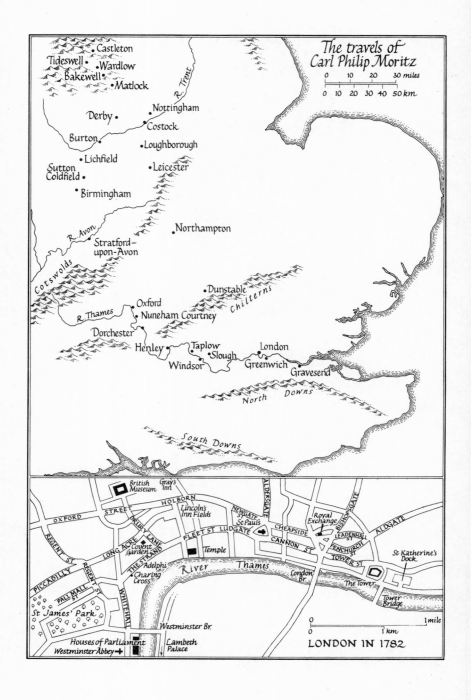

The travels of
Carl Philip Moritz

0   10   20   30 miles
0 10 20 30 40 50 km

Castleton
Tideswell   Wardlow
Bakewell
Matlock

R. Trent

Derby   Nottingham
Costock
Burton
Loughborough
Lichfield
Leicester
Sutton
Coldfield
Birmingham

R. Avon
Northampton
Stratford-
upon-Avon

Cotswolds

Dunstable
Oxford   Nuneham Courtney   Chilterns
R. Thames
Dorchester
Henley   Taplow   London
Slough
Windsor   Greenwich   Gravesend

North   Downs

South Downs

British   Gray's
Museum   Inn
HOLBORN   Lincoln's
OXFORD   STREET   Inn Fields   ALDERSGATE   BISHOPSGATE
NEWGATE   St Paul's   Royal   ALDGATE
LONG ACRE   FLEET ST   LUDGATE   CHEAPSIDE   Exchange
REGENT ST   DRURY LANE   Covent   Temple   CANNON ST   LEADENHALL   St Katherine's
Garden   ST   FENCHURCH ST   Dock
THE STRAND   TOWER ST
Adelphi   River   Thames   London
PICCADILLY   Charing   Br.   The Tower
Cross   Tower
PALL MALL   REGENT ST   Bridge
WHITEHALL
St James' Park
Westminster Br.
Houses of Parliament   Lambeth
Westminster Abbey   Palace

0   1 mile
0   1 km
LONDON IN 1782

JOURNEYS OF A GERMAN IN ENGLAND

CARL PHILIP MORITZ

A walking-tour of England in 1782

TRANSLATED AND INTRODUCED BY
REGINALD NETTEL

ELAND, LONDON
&
HIPPOCRENE BOOKS, INC., NEW YORK

Published by
ELAND BOOKS
53 Eland Road London SW11 5JX

First published in German in 1783

This translation first published by
Jonathan Cape in 1965
©Reginald Nettel

ISBN 0 907871 50 X
First issued in this paperback edition 1983
Reprinted 1986
All rights reserved

Printed and bound in Great Britain
by Redwood Burn Ltd, Trowbridge, Wiltshire

Cover illustration © Tony Ansell
Cover design © Patrick Frean
Index © Sarah Matthews
Map © Reginald Piggott

CONTENTS

Hill – The Prussian Ambassador, Count Lusi – Greek Pronunciation – Herr Leonhardi, Journalist and Freemason

declaration, Patriotic Ballads, Unpopularity of George III, High opinion of Frederick the Great of Prussia, The Lord Mayor's Show

EDITOR'S PREFACE

CARL PHILIP MORITZ published the first edition of his *Reisen eines Deutschen in England im Jahr 1782* in 1783, and a second, improved edition, from which this translation is taken, in 1785. In 1795 an English translation of the second edition was published under the title *Travels, chiefly on Foot, through several parts of England in 1782, described in Letters to a Friend.* It was said to be the work of an unknown English lady,* related to a person described in Moritz's book; and in the preface we read: 'The Editor has revised the translation, which, though far from being servile, or even literal, he thinks sufficiently faithful. Some little stiffness, it is possible, may still remain; but it has been the aim of the translator, without departing from the sense of the author, to express that sense in such a way as she supposed her author would have done, had he been of London, rather than of Berlin.'

Nobody would deny the wisdom of that, were it conscientiously done; but what do we find? Moritz was stopped on the road by a footpad who asked for a halfpenny to buy beer, but in the translation 'beer' is turned into 'bread'. In the next to last of Moritz's letters the words 'is a Jew' have become 'are a few'. On seeing the tombs in Westminster Abbey Moritz wrote (our translation), 'Gay's has a very touching inscription said to have been written by himself:

> Life is a jest and all things show it:
> I thought so once and now I know it.'

This becomes in the 1795 translation: 'The inscription on

* See p. 58.

13

Gay's tombstone is, if not actually immoral, yet futile and weak; though he is said to have written it himself:

Life is a jest, etc.'*

These are not mistranslations but deliberate alterations, typical of many in the book.

Nevertheless, the 1795 translation was reprinted in Mavor's *British Tourists*, vol. iv (1798); in Pinkerton's *Collections of Voyages*, vol. ii (1808); and again in 1881 under the title *Travels in England in 1782* by C. P. Moritz (Cassell's National Library, general editor, John Morley). The last reprint was issued by Humphrey Milford at the Oxford University Press in 1924; it was edited by P. E. Matheson, who has kept strictly to the text of 1795 but corrected a few misprints. He also added an introduction concerning Moritz and his English journey, and some notes pointing out the most obvious – but by no means all – of the mistranslations.

'Since everyone measures things outside himself with his own yardstick and looks at whatever he sees from his own point of view, it follows of course that I am no exception.' Thus runs the beginning of Moritz's own preface to the *Reisen*; it is unfortunate that this passage seems to have been interpreted as an invitation to vary his honest record of what he saw in England. Also, previous editors have failed to spot some mistakes which they would have seen had they visited the places Moritz described, as I have done.

I am obliged to the Librarian of the *Schloss* in Darmstadt for permission to photograph Moritz's original and to copy it for publication. I made a copy and a first translation which

---

* Moritz's original runs: *Sehr rührend ist Gays Grabschrift, die er sich selbst verfertigt haben soll:*
Life is a jest, etc.

I passed on to Hildegard Finger of Darmstadt, who has done the expert work of getting Moritz's exact meaning into English. Finally I restyled the English in order to remove any stiffness due to the unwanted persistence of German idioms in the English text. The result came out better than I had expected, for Moritz has a clear and uncomplicated mind which finds expression beautifully in English prose. I have kept his letters in order but inserted chapter headings as the reader will see, and since the book falls naturally into two parts – the first in London and the second on tour – I have made this division clear and provided between the two parts an interlude intended to help those whose knowledge of the English scene in 1782 may be otherwise confused by Moritz's many references to small matters not usually easy to come by in other books.

'And so', as Moritz said, 'if anyone should be minded to while away an hour over this book, for want of better occupation, I beg his attention to this brief preface and his indulgence for the narrator.'

R. N.

1965

Part One

IN LONDON

*

ONE

Arrival

Hamelin town's in Brunswick,
  By famous Hanover city;
The river Weser, deep and wide,
Washes its wall on the southern side;
A pleasanter spot you never spied.
                    ROBERT BROWNING

IN THE TOWN famous for the story of the Pied Piper there was born in 1757 a boy named Carl Philip Moritz. His father was a regimental oboist of strictly Pietist views, who treated his son harshly. After a short time as apprentice to a hatter in Brunswick the boy returned to his parents, who had meanwhile removed to Hanover. Here Carl was granted a free place in the Gymnasium or High School by favour of Prince Carl of Mecklenburg. Again he did not settle but left to join the Ekhoff theatrical company in Gotha. Ekhoff's part in the history of German romanticism was his transformation of stage speech from a stiff formal style to one more natural. This was the turning-point of Moritz's life. He was now living in the midst of the new style of art which we recognize as the period of *Sturm und Drang* – a stormy up-surge of creative effort under strong emotional pressure from within. Lessing had started the German appreciation of Shakespeare of which Moritz had heard something in Hanover, but the battle for truth to nature was still being fought in the German theatre, where Schiller was at this time still impoverished and subjected to a harsh tyranny.

Moritz learnt something of the art of declamation in the theatre and imbibed the true German patriotism then being established there – based not on political expediency but on the common feelings of men. There was a moral aspect of this: a concentration on truth to nature, which was a mani-festation of the will of God. While still with the theatrical company Moritz determined to study theology and entered his name at the University of Erfurt in 1776. He took his degree at the University of Wittenberg in 1777 and became a teacher of philosophy in Dessau. A year later he was in Potsdam teaching in the military orphanage, and he found also a post as a teacher of language in the High School of the Grey Cloister.

In Berlin he became friendly with Gedike, * a humanist like himself and an authority on the theory of education. These two men were both fond of walking and made at least one excursion together as far as Hamburg, walking all the way. Hamburg, being a port, was a meeting-place for ideas coming from abroad. There you could buy English news-papers and read the gossip of the London coffee-houses, learn of developments in scientific thought, philosophy, criticism and above all the new movement in English literature shown in the novels of Swift, Defoe, Fielding and Richard-son. Moritz was particularly fond of Goldsmith's *The Vicar*

* Friedrich Gedike. Prussian educationist, who with the sup-port of Baron Zedlitz introduced higher education in Berlin.

of Wakefield and almost worshipped Milton as a champion of liberty.

So when in 1782 he left his post in Berlin, what more natural than that he should take advantage of his freedom to visit England? He set out full of enthusiasm, accompanied by his friend Gedike as far as Hamburg, and when they parted on the quay Moritz promised to send his friend an account of his travels in England.

That series of letters has proved to be one of the most remarkable collections of evidence of the state of England in 1782 that we possess. Moritz arrived expecting all English geese to be swans and of course he found they were not, but he was a careful observer and a truthful recorder of manners and customs, political and religious life, the arts and the delightful country, which he never ceased to admire. As he went about the capital and the provinces he gained in understanding of the English and he was a man with a sensitive mind which responded in its style of expression. His prose takes on various hues according to the scene he has in his thoughts, and through it all we find him adding to the interest of his subject – building to a climax as his travels lead him on from one delight to the next.

This climax could not have been planned, for the letters were written on different days and sent off from different places. The literary merit of Moritz's book is that it demonstrates the value of his belief in truth as an aspect of nature. It translates into beautiful English, for it came from the mind of a man who, writing in German, was trying to capture the English way of thought. Moritz was a remarkably sympathetic writer.

He left Gedike on the quay in Hamburg and set sail for England. For fourteen days he tossed on the ocean; three of them he was seasick; then, out of the mist, loomed the land for sight of which all his perils had been undertaken, and thus he described it to Gedike:

On the Thames, May 31st

At last, dear Gedike, I am between the happy shores of the land it has been for so many years my ardent wish to see: of which I have dreamed so often. For several hours now the green hills of England have been discernible in the blue distance; now they stand revealed on both sides of the ship, like a double amphitheatre.

The sun breaks through the clouds, gilding the copses and the cornfields on the distant shores, while from the sea beside us protrude the points of two shipmasts – a fearful warning that we are sailing hard by the sandbank where so many luckless travellers have found their grave.

The land creeps ever closer; the danger of the voyage is over now and we can begin to rest easy in our minds. How wonderful to stand once more between visible limits after being tossed so long upon a vast expanse! How safe and cosy does the wanderer feel in his nightly inn and the seafarer in the long-sought harbour! For though a man may be surrounded by a vast horizon, though the monstrous sea is everywhere, yet he can think only of his immediate environment – of one small portion of the whole.

But it is a very superior portion of the whole of bounteous Nature which I see now. The Thames is dotted with many ships, large and small, sailing by or lying at anchor. The hills on either side are clothed in a green as mild and soft as ever I saw. The banks of the Elbe from which I came are as much surpassed by these as autumn is by spring. Everywhere about me I can see only fruitful land. The quickset hedges which enclose the cornfields give this country scene the aspect of a great majestic garden. Neat villages and pretty little towns lie here and there, with the graceful country houses of the gentry in between, all betokening a state of comfortable well-being.

Especially fine is the view towards Gravesend, cleverly built on the side of a slope and around which hill and valley, fields and hedgerows are pleasantly intermingled with the parks and country houses; and there on one of the highest hills stands a windmill, a prominent landmark seen by the sailors in its familiar setting from various points along the winding Thames.

But since no pleasure ever comes undiluted, so we on the quarterdeck are at the mercy of the weather. This is cold and turbulent. A long sharp shower has driven me into the cabin where I am trying to brighten a dull hour by writing to you about a pleasant one.

London, June 2nd

This morning the six of us who shared the captain's cabin asked to be put ashore a little before the ship reached Dartford, which is about ten English miles from London. This is the usual course taken by those who sail up the Thames, because of the astonishing mass of sea-borne traffic growing more and more congested as the city is approached. Often it takes several days for a ship to work a passage through those last few miles. Passengers who therefore wish to lose no time and to avoid such other inconveniences as frequent stops and buffeting by other craft, prefer to travel the last few miles by land, possibly in a post-chaise, the cost of which is not very dear, especially if three persons share the same vehicle, for then the three pay no more than one. This is allowed by Act of parliament.

A rousing cheer went up for us from the German crew of our ship, after the fashion they have copied from the

English sailors. The shore where we disembarked was white and chalky. We had to get to Dartford on foot, first going up a fairly steep hill which brought us straight from the river to our first English village. With this I was pleasantly surprised – with the neatness of its domestic architecture, red brick walls and flat roofs – especially when I compared these with the huts of our Prussian peasantry.

So we trailed along from one village to another like a caravan, each of us with his staff. Several people meeting us stared as if surprised by our appearance and manner of progress. We went by a small wood where a group of gipsies had encamped round a fire under a tree. The countryside grew ever more beautiful as we went our solitary way. The earth is not the same everywhere. How different did I find these living hedges, the green of them and of the trees – this whole paradisiacal region – from ours and all others that I have seen! How incomparable the roads! How firm the pathway beneath me! With every step I took I was aware I trod on English ground!

We breakfasted in Dartford where I saw my first English soldier, in his red uniform, with his hair cut short behind and combed forward in a fringe on his forehead. Also a couple of boys boxing in the street.

Then we separated so as to occupy two post-chaises – three of us in each, with a little inconvenience. To hire one costs a shilling a mile. These vehicles may be compared with our *Extraposten* because they may be hired at any time, but a post-chaise is built in a pattern both trim and light, so that you are hardly aware of it as it rolls along the firm well-made road. It has windows in front and at both sides, the horses are good and the postilions always drive at full trot. Our postilion had short hair, a round hat, brown coat of fairly fine cloth and a bunch of flowers at his breast. Every now and then, when he was making good speed, he turned and smiled at us as if to invite our approval.

All this time the gorgeous landscape, so delightful to my eyes, flew past with the speed of an arrow; up hill, down hill; into a wood, out of the wood — every few minutes; then another glint of the Thames with the masts of its ships and on again through fascinating towns and villages. I was much astonished at the great signboards hanging on beams across the street, from one house to another, at various spots. These somewhat resembled town gates — which at first I took them to be — but this is not so; they do no more than indicate the entrance to an inn.

So, with one vision after another in such quick succession as to put the mind in a whirl, we arrived near to Greenwich, and to

THE PROSPECT OF LONDON

It loomed out of a thick mist; St Paul's rearing above the multitude of smaller buildings like a huge mountain. The Monument — a tall, round column erected to commemorate the Great Fire of London — making a striking picture on account of its height and apparent slenderness.

As we drew nearer and nearer with ever greater speed the surrounding objects grew more distinct at every moment: Westminster Abbey, the Tower, a steeple of one church after another came into view. Soon we could distinguish the high round chimneys on the houses, which seemed to form an innumerable crowd of smaller steeples.

The road from Greenwich to London was actually busier than the most popular streets in Berlin, so many people were to be encountered riding, driving or walking. Already we saw houses on all sides, and all along the road at suitable distances lamp-posts were provided. What struck me particularly was the number of people on horseback wearing spectacles – some of them apparently quite young. We were stopped at least three times at turnpikes or barriers in order to pay toll, which in the end amounted to a few shillings, although the individual payments had been only in coppers.

Finally we arrived at the magnificent bridge of Westminster. To cross over this bridge is in itself like making a miniature journey, so varied are the sights. In contrast with the round, modern, majestic cathedral of St Paul's on the right there rises on the left the long medieval pile of Westminster Abbey with its enormous pointed roof. Down the Thames on the right can be seen Blackfriars Bridge, hardly less lovely than its neighbour upon which we ride. On the left bank of the Thames, beautified with trees, stand terraces, and among them the newly erected Adelphi Buildings. On the Thames itself pass forth and back a great swarm of little boats, each with a single mast and sail, in which people of all classes can be ferried across; and so the river is nearly as busy as a London street. Big ships are no longer to be seen, as they come no farther than London Bridge at the other end of the city.

We drove into the city by way of Charing Cross and the Strand, as far as those very Adelphi Buildings which offered so attractive a prospect from Westminster Bridge. My travelling companions – a pair of young Englishmen who had come with me in the post-chaise from the ship – had offered to find me a lodging that day in their neighbourhood.

Everything in the streets through which we passed seemed dark even to blackness, but nevertheless magnificent. I could not reconcile the outward appearance of London with that of any similar town I had ever seen, though it is remarkable that on my first entering Leipzig, five years ago, I received a similar impression, possibly by reason of the high houses which make the streets themselves dark, the numerous merchants' stores and crowd of people. In all these ways Leipzig resembled what I now see in London.

Leading from the Strand to the Thames run numerous delightful side-streets, of which the Adelphi Buildings make up by far the most beautiful. In this neighbourhood are to be found York Buildings, adjacent to which is George Street, where my two travelling companions lived. In these little streets leading down to the Thames there reigns – in contrast to the tumult of men, carriages and horses which pass up and down the Strand – a calm so pleasant that one may believe himself to be far away from the busy city which is yet so near.

It would be about ten or eleven o'clock when we arrived. After the two Englishmen had given me a breakfast of tea, bread and butter in their lodging, they went with me round the neighbourhood seeking accommodation for me, which eventually they found in the house of a tailor's widow, opposite their own, for sixteen shillings a week. It was lucky that they accompanied me, for I had with me neither a change of clothes nor clean linen from my trunk and I might have had difficulty in finding suitable accommodation.

It was an uncommon but very pleasant experience to find myself for the first time now among the English: among a people who spoke a different language, had different manners and a different climate, yet with whom I could communicate as if I had been brought up with them from boyhood. Certainly it is invaluable for a traveller to know the language of the country in which he finds himself. I was not at first completely at ease with it, so they in the house were somewhat puzzled at my speech, but the more I spoke, the more liking and interest I inspired.

I now occupy a large front room on the ground floor,

with carpets, mats, and very good furniture: the chairs are upholstered in leather and the tables are of mahogany. Adjoining this I have another large chamber. I can do just as I like, and I keep my own tea, coffee, butter and bread in a glass-fronted cupboard with a lock, which my landlady has provided for me.

The family consists of the housewife, her maid and her two small sons Jacky and Jerry (abbreviations of John and Jeremiah). The elder, twelve-year-old Jacky, is a very lively character and entertains me pleasantly, telling me about his school work and then looking to me to tell him of my German schooling. He says his *amo, amam, amas, ames* in the same sing-song tone our schoolboys use. Once, in his presence, I happened to be humming a merry tune: he stared at me in surprise and reminded me that it was Sunday. And so, not to give him a wrong impression, I answered that in the confusion of my journey I had forgotten what day it was.

TWO

London streets and people

London, June 2nd (continued)
AT MIDDAY today little Jacky took me to St James's Park, not far from here, and now it is your turn to learn something about this famous place.

ST JAMES'S PARK

This park is nothing more than a semi-circular avenue of trees enclosing a large area of greensward in the midst of which is a swampy pond.

Cows feed on the turf and you may buy their milk quite freshly drawn from the animal. In the avenues are seats on which to rest. If you come into the park from the Horse Guards' Parade, as you may do by way of several paths, the royal residence of St James's Palace is on the right. Although famous, it is one of the least significant buildings in London. Right at the lower end is the Queen's Palace, handsome and modern, yet looking very like a private house. For the rest, however, the neighbourhood of St James's Park contains some most magnificent buildings which greatly enhance the beauty of the place. In front of the semi-circle through which the avenues run is a large military parade-ground.

How little this compares with our *Tiergarten* in Berlin I ought not to say. If we think highly of St James's Park and other public places in London it may be because they have figured more often than ours in novels and other books. The very streets and squares of London are more world-renowned than most of our cities.

What, then, is there to recommend this rather second-rate park of St James's? It is the astonishing medley of people who take their evening walk there in fine weather. The finest promenades in our country are never so full as they are here, with dense crowds of people strolling up and down. It is the first time in my life that I have had the pleasure of mixing with such a concourse of people, most of whom are handsome and well-dressed.

Before I went to this park, however, little Jacky had taken me for another walk which, though needing little effort, proved to be extraordinarily stimulating. I went down the little street in which we live, in the direction of the Thames, and, nearly at the end of the street, descended a few steps which led to a Thames-side terrace pleasantly lined with trees.

From here I had the most beautiful view imaginable. Before me lay the winding Thames with the stately arches of its bridges – Westminster with its venerable Abbey lay to the right, while London with St Paul's curved along the bank of the river to the left. On the other side lay South-wark, now also regarded as a part of London. From this position I could see almost at a glance the whole of the city – at least that side of it which graces the Thames. Not far from where I stood, in this delightful quarter, had lived the famous actor David Garrick. No doubt I shall often take this walk during my stay in London.

At midday today my two Englishmen took me to a nearby eating-house where we paid a shilling for a little salad and roast meat, and gave nearly half of that sum also to the waiter – which must amount to about nine or ten groschen in our money and is yet regarded here as very cheap living! I shall dine at home in future, as I have already done this evening. I am now sitting by an open fire in my room, and so ends the first day I have spent in England. When I think of all the new experiences of this day, however, it is difficult to believe that it is only one!

London, June 5th

At last, dear Gedike, I am again settled, with my trunk and belongings here from the ship, which only arrived at its mooring yesterday morning. As I did not want to take my trunk to the Custom-house (which involves a great deal of trouble) I had to pay the Excise Officers who came aboard the ship. Having bribed one of these with two shillings, however, a second protested against their handing over the trunk until he had received a like amount, and so did the third. So the affair cost me six shillings, but I gave it willingly because the cost would have been even more if the trunk had been taken to the Custom-house.

Several porters were available by the bank of the Thames, one of whom lifted my heavy trunk on his shoulders with astonishing ease and for two shillings carried it until we found a hackney coach. In this we deposited the trunk and I got in with it. I did not have to pay anything extra for the carriage of the trunk; this is a great advantage of the English hackney coaches, that you may take what you will with you; so you save half as much, as you would have to pay a porter and ride yourself into the bargain. The witty cut-and-thrust of question and response among the common people here is

31

striking in its directness. When I arrived home with the coachman my hostess warned him not to overcharge me because I was a foreigner. 'But even if he weren't a foreigner I wouldn't overcharge him,' answered the man.

On account of my hasty departure from Hamburg I was unable to bring with me letters of recommendation to a merchant here, but these have now arrived and I am thus relieved of a great deal of anxiety regarding the changing of my money. What I have I can take with me back to Germany and the German correspondent of the London merchant will credit him with the amount I have drawn from him in English money. Otherwise I should have had to sell my Prussian Fredericks d'or at their weight value. (I received no more than eight shillings for some Dutch ducats which I had been obliged to sell in the meanwhile.)

A foreigner has nothing to fear from the Press Gang here provided he keeps away from suspicious places. Standing on dry land on Tower Hill, near the Tower of London, is a ship complete with masts and rigging. This is no more than an ingenious device for catching unwary visitors. Simple people who stand and stare at it – some of whom come from the country districts – are approached by a man who offers for a trifle to show them round the ship and explain everything to them. But as soon as they are aboard they are trapped, and, according to their circumstances, are either released or pressed for service as sailors.

A stranger, however, appreciates the sidewalks made of broad stones, running down both sides of the streets, whereon he is as safe from the terrifying rush of carts and coaches as if he were in his own room; for no wheel dares to encroach even a finger's breadth upon the footpath. Politeness requires that a lady, or other person to whom one wishes to show respect, should not always walk on one's right, as is our custom, but should walk on the side nearest to the wall, whether this be right or left, as this position is regarded as safer. You will never see a sensible man walking in the middle of the road except when he has to cross over, and even this is dangerous at Charing Cross and other places where several roads meet.

Especially in the Strand, where one shop jostles another and people of very different trades often live in the same house, it is surprising to see how from bottom to top the various houses often display large signboards with painted letters. Everyone who lives and works in the house sports his signboard over the door; indeed there is not a cobbler whose name and trade is not to be read in large golden characters. On one door after another it is not unusual to read: 'Foreign Liquors sold here' and 'Funerals undertaken here'. I have found 'Dealer in Foreign Spirituous Liquors' to be the most frequent inscription among them. It is said that the insatiable lust for brandy, especially among the common people, goes to fantastic lengths, and there is a phrase used by everybody – 'He is in liquor' – when they mean that he is drunk. In the terrific Gordon Riots here – recent enough to be still a current topic of conversation – more people were found dead beside the looted and emptied brandy casks than were killed by the musketry of the troops called in to quell the riot.

So far as I have seen in my two days going about London, there are no houses and streets here so beautiful as those in Berlin, but on all sides there are many more handsome and better dressed people. It gives me real delight, whenever I walk from Charing Cross along the Strand, and so on past St Paul's and the Royal Exchange, to meet so many people from the highest to the lowest class neatly and cleanly dressed. Not a man pushing a wheelbarrow but he has his white underclothing, and hardly a beggar can be espied who doesn't wear a clean shirt under his tatters.

It is surprising to see a funeral procession in such a bustling throng, when all are going about their business or pleasure with as much speed and eagerness as they can command. How they must jostle one another! English coffins are economically designed to fit the shape of the corpse – flat and broad on top, the middle part bowed and tapering from there almost to a point at the feet, for all the world like an oversize violin case.

A few bearers make their way as well as they can through the crowd and several mourners follow. As for the rest of the populace, they take no more notice than if a hay-cart were driving past. Burials of distinguished people may possibly be regarded differently.

Apart from this it seems to me that in a populous city such a funeral as this is all the more unseemly because of the indifference of the spectators and the little sympathy they show. The man being borne to his grave might never have belonged to the rest of humanity. In a small town or a village everybody knows everybody else and his name at least will be mentioned.

The influenza which I left behind me in Berlin I have encountered here again. Many are dying of it. As yet it is unusually cold for the time of the year so that I have to have my fire made every day. I must admit that the warmth from sea-coal burnt in an open firegrate comes out more comfortably than in our closed stoves; the look of the fire, too, brings pleasure. Only, one is obliged to avoid looking straight into it continuously, and now I can understand how from that habit there are so many young oldsters riding or walking about the English streets with spectacles on their noses, employing in the bloom of their youth a blessing for the senile.

Indeed, spectacles are sold in the shops under the slogan: 'the blessings of old age'.

I now invariably take my meals at home and, all in all, these are tolerably frugal. My usual dish for supper is pickled salmon – a very refreshing and satisfying food when eaten with oil and vinegar.

I would advise anybody who wants to drink coffee in England to mention beforehand how many cupfuls should be made from half-an-ounce, otherwise he will get an atrocious mess of brown water set before him, such as I have not yet been able to avoid in spite of all my admonitions. Their fine wheaten bread, along with butter and Cheshire cheese, suffice for my meagre midday meal. Here they content themselves generally with a piece of half-boiled or roasted meat and a few green cabbages boiled in nothing else but water, on which is poured a sauce concocted of flour and butter. This, I assure you, is the general way they prepare vegetables in England.

The slices of bread and butter given to you with tea are as thin as poppy-leaves, but there is a way of roasting slices of buttered bread before the fire which is incomparable. One slice after another is taken and held to the fire with a fork until the butter is melted, then the following one will be always laid upon it so that the butter soaks through the whole pile of slices. This is called 'toast'.

In particular I like their way of sleeping without a feather-filled bedcover. You lie between two sheets, the upper one covered with a light woollen blanket that warms you adequately without pressing. The cleaning of shoes is not done in the house but by a woman in the neighbourhood who makes this her trade. She collects the shoes from the house every morning, cleans them and brings them back for a fixed weekly payment. When the serving-maid doesn't

35

like me I occasionally hear her at the door calling me 'the German'. In the house I am called 'the gentleman'.

Quite sensibly I have given up driving. True, it costs less here than in Berlin. I can travel an English mile and back for one shilling whereas in Berlin I should have to pay at least a gulden. However, one saves a lot by walking if only one knows how to ask the way. It is a long way from my lodging in the Adelphi to the Royal Exchange – as far as from one end of Berlin to the other, and as far again from there to the Tower and St Katherine's, where the ships arrive on the Thames. I have already walked this way twice on account of my trunk being on the ship.

As it was dusk on the first evening when I returned from there I was astonished at the unusually good lighting of the streets, compared with which Berlin makes a pretty poor show. The lamps are lit while it is still daylight and are placed so close to each other that this ordinary street-lighting glows like a festive illumination. A German prince arriving for the first time in London actually believed that they had done it all especially for him!

London, June 9th, 1782

Today I preached for Pastor Wendeborn in the German Church on Ludgate Hill. *

Pastor Wendeborn is the author of *Die statischen Beiträge zur nähre Kenntnis Grossbrittaniens*, which has already proved of great service to me, so much so that I should like to advise anyone intending to travel to England to bring a copy of this book with him, especially as it can be carried in the pocket. Every bit of it contains useful information. And of course, since Herr Wendeborn has already lived for a long

* Dr G. F. A. Wendeborn (1742–1811), pastor of a German Lutheran Church on Ludgate Hill from 1770, and London reporter for the *Hamburger Korrespondent*.

time in England he has been able to make more accurate and extensive observation than anyone just passing through, as I am, or who has been there only for a short stay. With this book at hand it would be hard for anyone to miss anything noteworthy in or around London, especially as regards the system of government.

Herr Wendeborn lives in New Inn, near Temple Bar, in a peaceful atmosphere conducive to philosophy but not to idleness. He is well-nigh a naturalized Englishman and his library consists mainly of English books. Incidentally I should mention that he does not rent his apartment in the greater building of New Inn, but has bought it, just as have all the other residents in the building; and such a purchaser of a set of rooms – comprising, say, sitting-room and bedroom – is legally considered a property-owner – a householder with the right to vote at parliamentary elections, unless, like Herr Wendeborn, he is a foreigner. Nevertheless Herr Wendeborn was visited by Mr Fox when canvassing votes for his last election as Member of Parliament for Westminster.

At Herr Wendeborn's I saw for the first time a useful apparatus which seems not to be very well known yet in Germany – or at any rate not much used. This is a press operating by strong steel springs which makes a print from a written page on to a blank sheet, thereby serving the double purpose of saving the labour of transcription and providing a copy of the original handwriting. Herr Wendeborn uses this machine whenever he wishes to keep a copy of a manuscript he is sending away. It is made of mahogany and pretty expensive.

I suppose that the London habit of getting up late in the morning accounts for divine service not commencing until half-past ten. I missed Herr Wendeborn this morning and so had to ask the doorkeeper of St Paul's the way to the German Church where I was to preach. He did not know. I therefore asked at another church not far away and was there properly directed at last. After passing through an iron gate and along a lengthy passage I arrived finally at the church just in time. After the sermon I had to offer thanks for the safe arrival of our ship in London. The German clergy here dress just like the English, in long gowns with wide sleeves; into such a thing I was obliged to wrap myself. Herr Wendeborn wears his own naturally-curled hair combed up in front after the English manner; the other German clergymen I have seen wear wigs, as do many of the English clergy.

Yesterday I waited on our ambassador Count Lucy* and was pleasantly surprised at the simplicity of his mode of life. He lives in a small private house; his secretary lives upstairs, where I spoke with the Prussian Consul who was visiting him at the identical time. Downstairs to the right, on the ground floor, I was shown without delay into his Excellency's room without having to pass through an antechamber. He wore a blue coat with red collar and facings. Over a cup of coffee we discussed various learned topics; when I told him of the great dispute over '*Stacismus*' and '*Itacismus*', he declared himself, as a born Greek, in favour of 'Itacismus'.† He asked me to visit him whenever I wished, without ceremony, and assured me that I should always be welcome.

Herr Leonardi,‡ who has translated several well-known

* Lusi, Graf Spiredom von, Prussian ambassador 1781–8: scholar, soldier, diplomat.

† This controversy turned round the pronunciation of the Greek vowel η: whether it should be sounded like the English vowel i, or ē.

‡ Translator of *The School for Scandal* (Sheridan), *The Beaux Stratagem* (Farquhar), *The False Friend* (Vanbrugh), *Who's the Dupe?* (Hannah Cowley).

pieces from English into German – such as *The School for Scandal* (*die Lästerschule*) – lives here privately, employing himself as a skilful teacher of English to Germans and German to the English; acting, too, as English correspondent to the new Hamburg newspaper for an annual stipend. He is Master of a German lodge of Freemasons in London and representative of all the German Masonic Lodges in England, but I fear that this occupation brings him more trouble than profit since everyone applies to him. He is however a most obliging man and has already done me several favours. He understands very well the art of declaiming English verse and speaks the language almost as if it were his mother tongue. Also, he is married to an affectionate Englishwoman. I wished him the best luck in the world!

Now you shall hear something about that inimitable yet much-imitated place – Vauxhall!

THREE

The Pleasure Gardens

June 9th (continued)

YESTERDAY I visited Vauxhall for the first time.

It is not far from my lodging to Westminster Bridge, where many boats lie awaiting hire by all comers for a shilling or sixpence. So I was ferried all the way from there on the Thames to Vauxhall, passing Lambeth on the left, where the ancient palace of the Archbishop of Canterbury can be seen.

Vauxhall is really the name of a small village wherein the garden of this name is situated. On payment of a shilling for admission anyone may enter.

In so far as one can compare the lesser with the greater, I found on entering this original Vauxhall some actual similarity with our Vauxhall in Berlin: at any rate the walks, with statues at the far end, and the high trees which at times form a wood on either side, so resembled our Vauxhall that in my stroll I lulled myself into the pleasant belief that I was there, especially as I met several Berliners born and bred, like Herr Splittgerber, with whom I spent a most agreeable evening.

Here and there, especially in the little wooded plantations in this garden, you unexpectedly come upon the pleasant novelty of a statue of one of the famous English poets or philosophers – Milton, Thomson, etc. What delighted me most was the statue of the German composer Händel standing near the entrance to the garden, not far from the place where the music is performed.

This handsomely built stage stands in a little wood beneath a mass of trees, so that as soon as you enter the garden you are met with the sounds of vocal and instrumental music. Here may be heard famous women singers whenever you go.

Near to the stage, at the sides of the garden, are small alcoves with tables and seats for those who wish to dine. The paths in front of these are filled with people from every walk of life – as indeed are all the paths in the garden. I dined here with the Secretary of the Prussian Legation, also Herr Splittgerber and some other Berliners, and what astonished me most was the boldness of the lewd strumpets who came in by the half-dozen with their go-betweens, shamelessly begging one glass of wine after another for themselves and their hangers-on, which we dared not well refuse them.

An Englishman rushed past our alcove and when we asked him what he was looking for he answered in the most comical manner: 'I have lost my girl!' Which made us laugh, since he might in the same way have been looking for a glove or a walking-stick which he had mislaid somewhere.

Rather late in the night we saw yet another spectacle in one part of the garden. Here, by means of an ingenious machine, a curtain was operated to simulate audibly and visibly the effect of a waterfall sweeping down from a high rock. As everyone was crowding to this spot the cry went up

'Take care of your pockets!' – a sign that pickpockets had already had a successful haul.

The celebrated Rotunda especially interested me. This is a handsome round building in the garden glistening with resplendent chandeliers and large mirrors, and adorned all round with paintings and sculpture. Here, when tired of the bustle of the crowded pleasure-walks, one may meditate by the hour on these works of art.

Among them is one depicting the surrender of a besieged city. Look at it long enough and you will be driven to tears. The impression of distress, bordering on despair, as the beleaguered citizens await in fear the victors' decision regarding their fate, is so lifelike that, looking on the faces of the unfortunates – from that of the grey-headed man to that of the suckling held up by its mother, all begging for mercy – you become almost convinced that you are looking at no mere picture.

Here in the Rotunda are also to be found busts of leading English authors, placed around the side of the building; thus are Shakespeare, Milton and Dryden recalled to mind in a place of public entertainment. Even the common people learn to know these names and mention them with respect. In this Rotunda also is a stage where music is played on rainy evenings.

But enough of Vauxhall.

It is plain beyond all comparison that the classical English authors are more read than the German. German authors are hardly read outside learned circles except by a few of the middle class. Yet the common people of England read their English authors! You can tell it, among other things, from the number of editions of their works.

My landlady, who is but a tailor's widow, reads her

Milton and tells me that her late husband fell in love with her because of the good style in which she read that poet. This single example would mean nothing by itself, but I have spoken with more of the common people, all of whom know their English authors and have read some of their works. This improves the lower classes and brings them nearer to the higher, so that there are few subjects of general conversation among the latter on which the workers are not able to form an opinion. Among us Germans however I can think of no poet's name beyond Gellert's which comes readily into the minds of the common people.*

Even more is being done in England for the classical authors by issuing their works in cheap and convenient editions. They can be bought in any format, including pocket editions, according to choice. I have bought for two shillings an edition of Milton bound in calf, which I can carry easily in my pocket, and it seems to me also that those books most read are generally neatly bound before sale.

Second-hand dealers are occasionally to be met in the street who sell odd volumes of Shakespeare or other little literary wares for a penny or even for a halfpenny. I have bought both volumes of *The Vicar of Wakefield* for sixpence from such a man.

But I have seen from an advertisement in a book how our German literature is also appreciated in England. Under the title of *The Entertaining Museum, or complete circulating Library*, a list of all English authors is to be issued, and also translations of the most famous French, Spanish, Italian and, as the advertisement puts it, 'even German' novels!

* Christian Fürchtegott Gellert (1715–69). Popular poet and lecturer in Leipzig, who wrote to improve moral tone of the people. His novel *Die schwedische Gräfin* (after Richardson's *Pamela*) was the first German attempt at a psychological novel.

43

The price of the book is worthy of note because it indicates how readily books are available to the people. Everybody should be able to buy this book and so provide himself with a most desirable library without noticing the cost, says the advertisement, since a small volume will be issued each week at a cost of sixpence paper-covered, or ninepence bound in leather with the title on the spine. The twenty-fifth and twenty-sixth volumes of this enterprise contain the first and second parts of *The Vicar of Wakefield* which I have already bought (as I mentioned) from a perambulating dealer.

Probably the only translation from the German into English to make a literary stir is Gessner's *Death and Abel*, the translation of which has been oftener issued in England than the original was in Germany. * The eighteenth edition has now appeared, and, according to the Preface, comes from a woman. Klopstock's *Messiah* is not well received here; the translation is said to be too free, but I have not seen it. Herr Pastor Wendeborn has written a German Grammar for the English which is well spoken of, and it must not be forgotten that the writings of our Jakob Böhme are all to be had in English translation.

London, June 13th

Although I had so often heard of Ranelagh I had no very clear idea of it. I knew it was a garden, somewhat differently arranged than Vauxhall, but exactly how I did not know.

Yesterday I started out on foot to visit this resort of pleasure; I missed my way, however, and eventually found myself in Chelsea. There I met a man pushing a wheelbarrow, who not only directed me very politely but also spoke with me during the time he went with me. He asked

* Translated by Mary Collyer in 1761.

me from which country I came, and when I told him I was from Prussia, he inquired very eagerly about our King of Prussia and listened to many stories I told him about that monarch.

So at last I came to Ranelagh, and, after paying my half-crown at the entrance, asked the way to the garden door. This was pointed out to me and then, to my great astonishment, I found myself in a garden rather large but sickly in its aspect, unseemly, ill lit and sparsely inhabited. I had not been there long before a young lady who was likewise strolling about offered me her arm without introduction and asked me why I was going about all alone. It struck me at that moment that this could not possibly be the magnificent and much recommended Ranelagh! So, as I saw several people go through a door, I followed, hoping by that way to come out into the fresh air or at least to a change of scene.

But what a sight I saw as I came from the darkness of that garden into the glare of a round building lit with hundreds of lamps, surpassing in splendour and beauty any I had ever seen before! Everything here was circular. Above stood a gallery with private boxes; in one part of this gallery stood an organ and a well-built choir apse, from which poured forth music both vocal and instrumental. Round the building were set richly painted alcoves for those who wished to take refreshments. On the floor lay carpets surrounding four high black pillars containing ornate fireplaces where coffee, tea and punch were being prepared, and round all the circle tables were set with refreshments. Around these four high pillars all of fashionable London revolved like a gaily coloured distaff, sauntering in a compact throng.

On my entry I mixed with this crowd, and what with the constant changing of the faces around me (most of them strikingly beautiful), the illuminations, the majesty and splendour of the place, and the ever-present strains of music, I felt for a moment as a child would on first looking into a fairy-tale.

When I became tired of the crowd and of strolling round in a circle I sat down in one of the alcoves in order to take some refreshment, and from this vantage-point watched with ease the play and gathering of this happy carefree world. A waiter politely asked me what I should like and in a few minutes brought me my order. To my astonishment he would take no payment for the refreshments he had brought, and this I failed to understand until he explained that these had already been paid for with my half-crown entrance-fee and that I had only to say if I wanted more. If I wished, however, I might give him a small tip. This I did with great pleasure, since my half-crown could hardly pay for so much courtesy and entertainment.

I then went into the gallery and sat in one of the boxes, from which, like a solemn watcher of the world, I looked down on the concourse still turning round and round in circles. Some wore stars and symbols of noble orders, French hairdressing or official wigs. Old and young, nobility and commoners, I saw them all crossing and recrossing in a motley swarm. At my request an Englishman who had joined me pointed out the princes and peers who, with their huge stars, eclipsed the remainder of the company.

In one direction, some who wished to see and to be seen were going round in an everlasting circle, in another, a group of music-lovers had gathered to delight their ears in front of the orchestra; others were delighting their palates in a more substantial manner at the well-served tables. More, like myself, sat alone in the corner of a box in the gallery contemplating all these from above.

Every now and then I would compare for my own satisfaction the glitter of this scene with the darkness in the garden outside, in order to recapture some of the thrill I had enjoyed when I first entered the building. Well into the night I amused myself thus, until the throng began to thin out. Then I took a coach and drove home.

The company at Ranelagh looked superior to that at Vauxhall, for none of the lower class go there unless dressed in their best, so seeking to accommodate themselves to the prevailing social tone of the place. At least, I saw no one in all that throng who did not wear silk stockings. The poorest families make an effort to go to Ranelagh at least once a year, my landlady assures me; she herself always fixes a day in the year when without fail she will be ferried to Ranelagh. Moreover, the expense is not so great in Ranelagh as in Vauxhall if you take into account the cost of refreshments. Anyone who wants to dine in Vauxhall – as most of them do – can be charged half a guinea for a very sparing meal.

FOUR

Government

I HAD ALMOST FORGOTTEN to tell you that I have already been in the Houses of Parliament. This however is important, for if I had seen nothing but these while in England my journey would not have been wasted.

I have personally concerned myself very little in politics, since with us Germans it is hardly worth the trouble, yet I ardently desired to attend a sitting of Parliament and am glad to say that my wish was soon gratified.

One afternoon, about three o'clock, which is about the time when parliamentary sittings start, I asked the way to Westminster Hall and an Englishman very courteously directed me there. In this manner one may easily find one's way all over London, for anyone who has the ability to make himself understood may ask whom he pleases.

Westminster Hall is a huge Gothic building, its roof supported not by pillars but by misshapen angels' heads carved in wood and projecting from each side-wall.

Going through this long hall and mounting a few steps

at the end, you may pass down a dark passage and finally arrive at the House of Commons. This chamber has a pair of great double doors at floor level. Ascending a little staircase, however, you come to the strangers' Gallery overhead.

When I mounted these stairs for the first time and arrived at the parapet, I saw a very respectable man standing there dressed all in black, whom I asked if I might be allowed to go into the gallery. He replied that unless I were introduced by a Member of Parliament I could not be admitted. As I had not the honour of knowing a Member of Parliament, however, I turned and began to descend the stairs much disappointed. On the way down I heard something about a bottle of wine, apparently addressed to me but which I was utterly unable to comprehend until I arrived home, when my landlady explained that the well-dressed man wanted me to slip two shillings or half-a-crown into his hand to buy a bottle of wine.

This I did on the following day, when that very same man who had previously turned me away now opened the door – after I had pressed a mere couple of shillings in his hand – and personally recommended me to a place in the gallery with the utmost courtesy.

Then, in this rather unimposing building, rather like a chapel, I saw for the first time the whole English nation gathered together by representation. The Speaker, an elderly man, sat right opposite to me in a raised chair. He wore a full-bottomed wig, a black gown, and had his hat on his head; the chair much resembled a small pulpit except that it had no reading-desk upon it. In front of this chair stood a table, like an altar, at which sat two black-gowned men called clerks, and on this table lay a great gilded sceptre near the rolls of parchment which contained the Acts of Parliament. This sceptre is removed to a place under the table whenever the Speaker leaves his chair, which he does every time the House resolves itself into committee by which they mean an inquiry or discussion; during this time he lays aside his power and authority. As soon as the discussion is over, however, someone tells the Speaker, 'Now you can take the chair again', and the sceptre is replaced on the table before him.

The benches for the members of Parliament stand round the sides of the chamber under the gallery. They are covered with green cloth and so arranged that back benches are raised higher than those in front, like the choir-stalls in our churches, so that anyone addressing the House can always see over the heads of those sitting in front of him. Similarly with the benches in the gallery. Members keep their hats on but spectators in the gallery remove theirs.

Members of the House of Commons wear no special clothing. They enter the House in greatcoats, boots and spurs! It is not unusual to see a Member stretched out on one of the benches while the rest are in debate. One Member may be cracking nuts, another eating an orange or whatever fruit may be in season; they are constantly going in and out. Whenever one of them wishes to leave the chamber he stands first before the Speaker and makes him a bow, just like a schoolboy begging permission of his teacher.

Members address the House without any stiffness of speech. One of them simply rises from his seat, takes off his hat, turns towards the Speaker (to whom all speeches are directed), holds his hat and stick in one hand while he gesticulates with the other.

Whenever one of them speaks badly or the matter of his speech lacks interest for the majority, the noise and laughter are such that the Member can hardly hear his own words. This must be a very fearful time for him. It is amusing when the Speaker calls out from his chair, like a school-master appealing against disorder: 'To order! To order!' Often without attracting much attention.

During the course of a good, purposive speech, however, absolute stillness reigns, and one Member after another shows his approval by shouting 'Hear him!' – a cry often taken up by the whole House, making so much noise that the Speaker is often again interrupted by this shout of approval. Yet notwithstanding its inconvenience this shout is always a great encouragement and I have often observed how a Member who had begun with little confidence, speaking without much spirit, would warm up under such incitement and end with a flashing display of oratory.

As all speeches are addressed to the Speaker they begin with the word 'sir', whereupon the Speaker lifts his hat slightly but immediately puts it on again. This 'sir' is often used also in the course of the address and serves to help any-one who has lost his memory; for if he says 'sir' and with it makes a short pause, he can think of what is to follow. I have seen one obliged to draw a sort of plan out of his pocket, as at a loss, like a candidate hesitating in his sermon, but other-wise a parliamentary speech is never read. These speeches have their stock phrases, as 'whereof first consideration must be taken in this House', and the like.

On the first day I was there an Englishman who sat next to me in the gallery pointed out to me the best-known Members of Parliament, such as Fox, Burke, Rigby, etc., all of whom I heard address the House. They were debating whether some material reward should be given to Admiral Rodney in addition to his elevation to the peerage. In the course of the debate young Lord Fielding took Mr Fox to task for having, as a Minister of State, opposed the election of Admiral Hood as Member for Westminster.

Fox was sitting on the Speaker's right, not far from the table whereon the gilded sceptre lies. He now took his stand so near the table that he could reach it with his hand and was able to bang his fist on it with many a violent blow, thus giving force to his speech. He defended himself against Lord Fielding by insisting that he voted in the election referred to, not as a Minister, but in his capacity as a private citizen, in which capacity he had given his vote to another candidate – Mr Cecil Wray. When the King appointed him – Fox – Secretary of State, they made no bargain regarding his rights as a private voter, nor would he have engaged in such a barter anyway. I cannot describe to you with what fire and eloquence he spoke, and how the Speaker in his chair continually nodded approval with his great bewigged poll while all shouted 'Hear him! Hear him!' and when it seemed he was about to come to an end called out 'Speak yet!', and in this wise he continued nearly two hours.

Rigby thereupon made a short but witty speech to point out how little provision the bare title of Lord or Lady made without money, and closed with the Latin phrase: *Infelis pauperas quia ridiculos miseros facit*, after having observed however that inquiry should first be made to ascertain if Admiral Rodney had recently received any considerable prize-money, for in that event he would not need a further grant of money. Since then I have been to the Houses of Parliament almost every day and find the entertainment there to be satisfying beyond most other.

Fox is still much beloved of the people, despite his having been the cause of Admiral Rodney's recall. Yet I have myself heard Fox speak in highest praise of the Admiral. Charles James Fox is dark, small, thickset, generally ill-groomed and looks rather like a Jew; nevertheless he is well-informed and his political sagacity is evident in his eyes. I have often heard it said here: 'Mr Fox is cunning like a fox.' Burke is a well-built man, tall and straight but already looking somewhat elderly. Rigby is very fat, with a hearty red complexion.

I was much shocked by the open abuse which Members of Parliament flung at each other. For example, one Member ended his speech and another rose immediately and commenced with the phrase: 'It is quite absurd', etc., 'what the Right Honourable Gentleman has argued.' (For with this title do Members of the Lower House honour each other.) In conformity with parliamentary procedure, however, nobody says to another Member's face that he has spoken like a fool, but turns to the Speaker in the customary way and says, as though addressing the Speaker: 'The Right Honourable Gentleman has talked a lot of nonsense.'

It is very funny to see one Member speaking and another making the appropriate gestures, as I noted being done on one occasion by a worthy old burgess afraid to speak himself but who emphasized his neighbour's sentences with so many gestures that his whole body was in motion.

The gist of the debate is often lost in bickering and misunderstanding between each other. If they go on too long and become tiresome a general cry goes up: 'The question! The question!' which must often be repeated many times because both parties invariably want to have the last word. However, the question is at last put and the Speaker says: 'All in favour say "Ay"; all against say "No".' Then one hears a confused shriek of 'ay' and 'no' together and the Speaker says: 'It seems to me there are more "ayes" than "noes",' or *vice versa*. Then all spectators must leave the gallery and voting starts in earnest. Members look up at the gallery and shout, 'Withdraw!' until all spectators have left the room. Then they are locked in a room downstairs until the voting is over, after which they may return to the gallery. It greatly surprised me to see apparently well-conducted Englishmen pushing and shoving as soon as the door was reopened after the voting, in order to get the best seats in the gallery. Two or three times we were sent out of the gallery in this way and later allowed to return.

The spectators include people of all ranks and there are always ladies among them. A couple of shorthand-writers sat not far from me, trying stealthily to take down the words of the speakers, which can be read in print the same night. These reporters are presumably paid by the editors of the newspapers. There are a few regular visitors to Parliament who pay the doorman a guinea for the whole session. I have seen some Members of Parliament also take one of their young sons to sit with them in the House.

It has been proposed that a gallery should be erected in the House of Lords, but this has not been put into effect. There the business is conducted with more ceremony and decorum. Anyone who wishes to observe mankind, however, and study human nature in the raw, should go to the House of Commons.

Tuesday was hanging-day. It was also polling-day. And as I could not see them both I naturally decided on the latter. I only heard in the distance the death-bell tolling for the sacrifice to Justice.

Accordingly I shall now describe

A PARLIAMENTARY ELECTION

The cities of London and Westminster each send two members to Parliament. Fox is one of the two members for Westminster; the other seat is vacant and needs to be filled, for which reason that same Cecil Wray * whom Fox had previ-

---

* Sir Cecil Wray (1734–1805): see Interlude, p. 81.

ously opposed to Admiral Hood has now been publicly nominated.

Sometimes, when there is an opposition candidate, bloody heads have been seen; but here the election is already as good as settled, since those who were to have voted for Admiral Hood have withdrawn, knowing beforehand that nothing can come of it.

The vote was to be taken in Covent Garden – a big open-air market-place – and so a scaffold had been erected for the voters in front of the entrance to a church named St Paul's (but not to be confused with the Cathedral). The voters, dressed in red cloaks and carrying white sticks, sat on benches erected one above another on an inclined slope. The President sat on a chair. The whole of it was, however, only knocked together with wooden posts and planks. In front of this scaffold, where the benches ended, were laid mats on which those could stand who were to address the people. In the area before all this had gathered a crowd of people mainly of the lowest class. The orators bowed low to this rabble and always addressed them as 'gentlemen'. Mr Cecil Wray had to step forward and promise these 'gentlemen' with hand on heart that he would faithfully perform his duties as their representative in Parliament. He also apologized to them for not having waited upon them in their houses, as was their due; this, he explained, was on account of his long journey and illness. As soon as he began to speak, the whole crowd was as still as the raging sea becomes after a storm, and all shouted, 'Hear him!' and as soon as he had ended his address a great 'Hurrah!' rose up from every throat, and everyone – even the dirtiest coalheaver – waved his hat.

Mr Wray was then formally elected by the deputies on the stage, after which a man stepped forward and, in a well-delivered speech, wished the people and their new member all prosperity. He had indeed great skill in oratory and they knew it; so much so that a carter standing near me said: 'He speaks very well!'

Small boys hung on the railings and lamp-posts, listening to the speech with as much attention as if it were being addressed to them, and showed their appreciation at the end with a lusty 'Hurrah' and by waving their hats over their heads just like their elders.

And at this all the famous orators of ancient Rome came to my mind – Coriolanus, Julius Caesar and Antony. And though these things may be only an illusion – a mere political conjuring trick – yet they can by themselves inspire a fancy of the heart and spirit.

My dear friend, when one sees here how the lowliest carter shows an interest in public affairs; how the smallest children enter into the spirit of the nation; how everyone feels himself to be a man and an Englishman – as good as his king and his king's minister – it brings to mind thoughts very different from those we know when we watch the soldiers drilling in Berlin.

When Fox, who was one of the voters, drove up in his carriage at the start of the election, he was received with a rousing shout. Then, when the proceedings were nearly over, the people took it into their heads to hear him speak, and all cried 'Fox! Fox!' I, too, shouted along with them and he had to step forward and make a speech simply because they wanted to hear him. He confirmed before the people what he had said in Parliament: that he had taken no part in the election as a Minister of State, but had only exercised his right as a private citizen – the right to vote.

When all was over, the disposition of the English people showed itself in all its vigour. Within a few minutes the whole scaffold – benches, chairs and all – was smashed to bits, and the mats with which it had been covered torn into a thousand long strips. With these they formed a circle, enclosed within it anyone who came in the way, and drew them along in triumph through the streets.

Here in England everyone – even to the humblest – holds dearly in his mind the name which only poets mention in Prussia: the name of Fatherland. 'I'll shed every drop of my blood for my country!' says little Jacky in our house, and he is barely twelve years old! Love of their homeland and warlike valour are the common themes of their ballads and folksongs, sung in the streets by women selling them for a few farthings. Only lately our Jacky brought one home telling the story of a courageous admiral who continued in command even though he had had both legs shot away and had to be supported. Yet the scorn of the people for their king goes to astonishing lengths. 'Our King is a blockhead!' I have often heard said, while at the same time they praise the King of Prussia to the sky. He has a small head, they say, but it has a hundred times more sense in it than the King of England's fat head. Indeed the respect for our monarch is so pronounced in some of them that they earnestly wish he were their king. They only wonder at the great multitude of soldiers he keeps, and that so many of them are quartered in Berlin, whereas in the whole City of London not even one troop of the King's Guard may be seen.

A few days ago I saw the Lord Mayor's Show in London. He drove in a huge gilded coach with an astonishing train of coaches following, in which sat the other magistrates and aldermen of the City of London.

But enough!

FIVE

Information and entertainment

London, June 17th

HAVING STRUCK OUT in a different direction through London every day, I am now of the opinion that I am pretty well coming to an end of my perambulations. After this I want to travel farther afield and in a few days, God willing, breathe once more some clean air, for I have long been tired of this everlasting coal-smoke.

It is true that, taken on the whole, London's buildings are not so fine as those of Berlin, but London has a greater number of large open spaces called squares, surpassing in grace and symmetry our *Gen d'armes Markt, Denhöfchen* and *Wilhelmsplatz*.

These London squares contain the most splendid houses in London and in the midst of each is a round green lawn set about with railings. It usually has a statue in its centre. Those statues I have seen were equestrian and gilt. In the central round patch in Grosvenor Square a little wood is planted instead of a lawn.

One of the longest but most pleasant ways I have walked is from Paddington to Islington, where you can see on the left a fine view of the near-by hills, with the village of Hampstead on one of them, and on the right an ever-unfolding prospect of the streets of London. It is dangerous to walk alone here – especially in the afternoon and evening – for only last week a man was robbed and murdered on this road.

But let us turn to something else!

THE BRITISH MUSEUM

I have made the acquaintance of Pastor Woide, who is associated with the British Museum and gave me the opportunity to see it one day before it closed. But for this favour I should have had to give a fortnight's notice before being admitted. So quickly was I conducted through this museum, however, that I saw merely the rooms, glass cases and book repositories: not the true British Museum. The visitors were of all classes and both sexes, including some of the lowest class; for, since the Museum is the property of the nation, everyone must be allowed the right of entry. I had with me Herr Wendeborn's guide-book, which at least made me familiar with some of the special exhibits such as the Egyptian mummies, a head of Homer and a few other things. When the rest of the company saw that I had this book they gathered round me and I taught these English from Herr Wendeborn's book what they might see in their own museum! The custodian showed a scornful astonishment at this. Passing through all these rooms in one hour, you are astonished by the huge collection of treasures – of natural curiosities, antiquities and examples of learning which it would take a man at least a year to see and a lifetime to study. I have been told that some classes of subject may be far more comprehensively studied elsewhere, but, taken as a whole, and for sheer bulk, this collection has no equal.

Theologians travelling through like to be shown the old Alexandrian MS in order to see with their own eyes whether the phrase: 'There are three who bear witness' is there or not. *

Pastor Woide† lives not far from Paddington, in a very salubrious quarter on the edge of the town, where he breathes cleaner and fresher air than in the city. Although well known as a learned authority on Oriental languages, he is nevertheless a sociable and not unworldly man.

THE HAYMARKET THEATRE

Last week I went twice to an English theatre. On the first occasion *The Nabob*, by the late Samuel Foote, was played, and the afterpiece was a comic opera called *The Agreeable Surprise*, which certainly lived up to its name. On my next visit I saw *The English Merchant*, which is well known in its German translation under the title *Die Schottländerin, oder das Kaffeehaus*.

I have not visited Covent Garden or Drury Lane theatres because they are closed in summer. The best actors are travelling in the country from May to October and act only in the winter. With few exceptions the players whom I saw were nothing extraordinary.

* 1 John v. 7.

† Charles Godfrey Woide, D.D., F.S.A., F.R.S. (1725–90), Preacher at Dutch Chapel Royal in St James's Palace. Assistant librarian at British Museum from 1782. In charge of Hebrew and Arabic MSS. One of his two daughters may have been responsible for the first translation into English of Moritz's *Reisen eines Deutschen in England*.

It costs five shillings for a seat in a box, three shillings in the pit, two shillings in the circle and one shilling in the gallery; and the gallery certainly makes the most noise for its shilling. I sat in the pit, which slopes upwards from the orchestra to the far end and is filled from top to bottom with benches. Every moment a rotten orange came whizzing past me or past my neighbour; one hit my hat, but I dared not turn round for fear one hit me in the face.

Oranges are eaten practically everywhere in London, for they can be bought as cheaply as one or even two for a halfpenny. In the theatre I was charged sixpence for a single orange!

In addition to pelting from the gallery there is no end to their shrieking and banging with sticks until the curtain goes up. I have seen a tall baker's boy reaching over the rails and beating with his stick on the outside of the gallery with all his might, visible to everyone but quite unabashed. I sometimes also heard people in the circle quarrelling with those in the gallery.

Behind me in the pit sat a young fop who continually put his foot on my bench in order to show off the flashy stone buckles on his shoes; if I didn't make way for his precious buckles he put his foot on my coat-tails.

In the boxes sat servants of the gentry, who dared not look out or let themselves be seen for fear of being pelted with orange peel.

In Foote's *The Nabob* are local and personal satires; quite lost, I fear, on a stranger. A Mr Palmer played the Nabob – a silly fool with a fondness for slander – suddenly become immensely rich and much sought after by cranks – natural scientists, Quakers and who knows what else – all seeking his membership. Well, he is admitted to the Society of Natural Scientists and given a highly ridiculous speech to deliver. This he does so mockingly that it is heard in bewilderment. Two scenes, one with the Quakers and the other with the Society of Natural Scientists (who sat at a green table with their secretary making a careful inventory of the Nabob's ridiculous presents), were highly successful. One of the last scenes went over best; this was where one of the Nabob's old schoolfellows visited him and addressed him unceremoniously by his Christian name; but to all his schoolfriend's questions, as for example: 'Don't you know me any more?' 'Do you remember the trick we played on——, the fight we had when we were boys?' the Nabob replied with a frigid 'No sir.'

The after-piece *The Agreeable Surprise** proved a most comical farce with the universal trick of making a schoolmaster laughable on the stage. This is very natural since English schoolmasters are no less pedantic than others. The actor who played the part of the Nabob's schoolfellow in the preceding piece here played the schoolmaster with equal conviction and original humour. His name is Edwin†; he is certainly the best actor I have seen in London.

The schoolmaster is in love with a country wench named Cowslip and declares his affection in a very odd style, compounded of mythological-grammatical affectation. Among other fooleries he sings her the following air in a paroxysm of rapture which melts his soul in sentiment; in the process he starts with the Latin conjugations and ends with the declensions and genders:

> Amo, amas,
> I love a lass,
> She is so sweet and tender,

* *The Agreeable Surprise*, comic opera by John O'Keefe, music by Dr Arnold.

† John Edwin the Elder (1749–90).

It's sweet Cowslip's grace
In the nominative case
And in the feminine gender.

He sings the last two lines especially with an exaggerated delicacy. Yet this actor, Edwin, keeps a good-humoured expression through all his comic roles, different from anything I have seen in any other comedian, which makes his characters doubly interesting despite his absurdity. Nothing could equal the tone of self-satisfaction with which he answered one who asked him if he was a scholar. 'Why,' he said, 'I am a master of scholars!' A Mrs Webb* played the part of a cheesemonger – a common woman – so naturally that I have never seen its equal. Her massive body and whole external appearance, however, made her as if cut out for the part.

Poor Edwin, acting the part of the schoolmaster, will soon inevitably sing himself hoarse at the rate he is going on, for he has often to repeat two or three times his declensions-and-conjugations air, if the occupants of the gallery choose to shout 'Encore!' Then he has to make a grovelling bow, thanking them for the honour!

The funniest touch in the comedy was a lie which became more and more enormous as the plot went on, keeping the audience in almost constant laughter. The piece is not yet printed or I should have enjoyed translating it.

The English Merchant or *Die Schottländerin*† I have seen much better performed in Germany than here. In particular Herr Fleck in Hamburg acted the part of the English Merchant with far more interest and conviction than did a certain Aicken here in London. Aicken showed little or nothing of the originality of Freeport, but by his measured speech and gait tried to make him into a gentleman.

* Mrs Webb (d. 1793): pleasant voice and stout figure.
† Founded on *L'Écossaise* by Voltaire.

The old and trusty servant who was ready to lay down his life for his master – he too had the grave walk of a minister. Even Mr Palmer, who had played the part of the Nabob, played the newspaper reporter's part too slowly. All said he made the part too refined, besides which he was personally too imposing for the part.

Amelia was played by an actress making her first appearance and whose consequent timidity caused her to speak so low that she could not be heard in all parts of the theatre. 'Speak louder! O, speak louder!' sang out a lout from the gallery; and for a short time she complied. Those sitting near me in the pit were lavish with their applause; at the shortest and least comprehensible speech several voices would shout 'Very well!' so long as it was effectively delivered, as if they were connoisseurs admiring some masterstroke of histrionic art. In consequence their 'Very well' is of little value.

The Agreeable Surprise was repeated and I saw it with satisfaction the second time. It has become a popular play and is always announced as 'The favourite musical Farce'. The theatre seemed to me to be somewhat bigger than that in Hamburg and on both occasions was very full.

So much for the English theatre!

SIX

English customs and education

London, June 17th (*continued*)

NOW FOR SOMETHING about pedagogics.

I have seen the regulation of what is called in this country an 'academy'. In London are many such places, but basically they are no more than small boarding-establishments for children and young people set up by private persons.

One of the two Englishmen with whom I travelled to this country introduced me to Mr Green, who lives in the Paddington district and has there an educational institution for twelve young people. As with our Herr Kampe this number is never exceeded. A similar plan is adopted by others.

Going in, I saw over the door a large signboard bearing the words: 'Mr Green's Academy'. As I was a foreigner Mr Green received me in a very friendly manner and showed me his classroom, furnished with benches and a large chair, just like our public schools in Germany.

He had for assistant teacher a young clergyman who was sitting in the chair giving a lesson in Latin and Greek. Such an assistant is called an usher, and is usually a downtrodden creature – a drudge – just as he is described in *The Vicar of Wakefield*. As we stepped into the room he was listening to the boys declining their Latin in the old humdrum way, and it rang strangely in my ears when I heard, for example, the Latin *'viri'* pronounced as we should spell it in German, *'weirei'* – of the man; *'weiro'* – to the man, etc. They did the same thing later with the Greek – pronounced the words in the English way.

At midday Mr Green invited us to dine; and there I made the acquaintance of his very attractive young wife, who treated the children in such a way that I guessed she contributes more than anyone to their education in this little institute. The boys had only water to drink. Mr Green gets no more than thirty pounds a year for each boarder and complained that this was too little. The highest charge possible would be about forty or fifty pounds.

I told him about our improvements in the art of education and mentioned also the dignity of the teacher and suchlike matters. He listened to me attentively but seemed to have little notion himself on the matter. Before and after the meal the Lord's Prayer was offered up in French, as elsewhere, thus killing two birds with one stone by taking advantage even of this opportunity to practise a language. Later I told him my opinion of this sort of thing, which he didn't seem to take amiss.

After the meal the boys were free to play in a very restricted yard. Such accommodation is the very *ne plus ultra* of playing-space during the hours of recreation in most

66

London academies. Mr Green has also a garden at the end of the town, however, where he sometimes takes them for a walk.

In the afternoon Mr Green gave them lessons himself in writing, arithmetic and French, which they learnt readily under him; especially the writing, in which the young English certainly excel ours – probably because they need to learn only one sort of script. Soon the midsummer holidays will be here when the children go home for four weeks from all the academies; so they each have to make a careful copy of a written model to show to their parents – for that is what their parents want most to see. The boys must learn by heart all the rules of syntax.

All these schools should really be called 'boarding-schools', i.e. schools in which meals are provided. A few keep this name and these are often of more reputation than those which go by the much-vaunted name of 'academy'. Clergymen with low stipends generally run such schools – either in town or in the country – and adult foreigners can attend them in order to learn the language. Mr Green charges two guineas a week for board, lodging and English lessons. Anyone who wants to become perfect in his English, however, will do best by going well into the country and there living in the house of a clergyman who keeps a boarding-school. There he will hear nothing spoken but English and can learn it from old and young alike.

England has few great schools apart from the two universities of Oxford and Cambridge. In London there are two public schools: Westminster School and St Paul's School. The rest are private schools offering a sort of family upbringing which is certainly the most natural form of education if it can be kept so. A few so-called 'grammar-schools' are to be found here and there notwithstanding, where the teacher receives a salary in addition to the fees paid by the pupils.

Boys big and little are to be seen about the streets of London dressed in long blue coats reaching down to the feet and with white cravats like a preacher. These boys are from a charity school which takes its name from their dress – Blue Coat School. Singing in the streets by the choristers – usual in Germany – is not done here at all. Indeed the traffic on the streets – walking, riding, driving – would make it hardly practicable. Parents, even those not well off, seem to be kind and indulgent and do not crush the spirit of the young with blows and curses so much as ours do. Children should learn to set a value on themselves early in life; yet our lower classes bring up their children to accept that same slavery under which they themselves groan.

Notwithstanding all the vagaries of fashion, English boys remain true to nature until a certain age. What a contrast when I think of our six-year-old, pimpled, pampered Berlin boys, with great hair-nets and all the paraphernalia of an adult, even to being dressed in lace-trimmed coats, and compare these with the English boys in the flower of youth – lithe, red-cheeked, with open-breasted shirts, hair cut and curling naturally! Here in England it is unusual to meet a blotchy-faced boy or young man, or one with deformed features and disproportionate limbs. Were it so in Berlin a really handsome man would not be so conspicuous.

This free and natural dress is worn until they are eighteen or twenty. Then it is discontinued in the higher classes, but is retained among the common people. The upper-class young men then have their hair dressed, curled with hot irons, wear a thick pigtail and sprinkle half their backs with powder. I have to stay longer under the hands of my English hairdresser than I ever did under a German one, and sweat under his hot irons, with which he curls my hair from bottom to top in an effort to make me pass for an Englishman. (*O tempora, O mores!*) I should mention here that English hairdressers are also barbers, but shave very badly. Yet I think this business more suitable for them than for the surgeons who shave us in Germany. It is incredible how the present-day Englishmen Frenchify themselves. All they want to complete the job are hair-nets and swords, which I at least have not seen any of them wearing in a public street. Nevertheless they go to Court with them.

In the mornings they affect a sort of negligé called 'morning dress'. This means hair undressed and set in curlers, tail-coat and top-boots. In Westminster the morning lasts until about four or five in the afternoon, when first they dine and then arrange their supper and bedtime accordingly. Breakfast is generally taken at ten in the morning. The farther you go from the Court towards the City, however, the more middle-class they become. There they dine usually at three o'clock, or in effect as soon as the business is over on 'Change.

Formal dress is therefore not yet worn and the usual summer dress is a short, white waistcoat, black breeches, white silk stockings and a tail-coat generally of dark-blue cloth – so dark that it looks almost black. Dark colours serve them best. For a formal occasion they wear black. Officers do not go in uniform but dress as civilians, distinguishing themselves merely by a cockade in their hats.

As soon as the English are groomed and are wearing their cravats they seem to grow delicate and warn each other about the danger of catching cold. 'You'll catch cold,' they say, if you are only sitting in a draught or if you are not dressed warmly enough.

Conversation in summer usually turns on whether this

acquaintance or that is in the country or in the town. This indeed is natural, since nearly half the town-dwellers are gone into the country in summer; and there I shall soon go too, even though I am not an inhabitant of London.

Electricity is the plaything of the English. Anyone who can air views about it is sure to make a stir. So it is with a certain Herr Katterfelto, who passes himself off as a Prussian Colonel of Hussars, speaks bad English and understands, besides electricity and a few other tricks of physics, a little of the art of conjuring. By this – at least according to the papers – he bewilders the whole public. Almost every newspaper prints verses on the great Katterfelto, written, it is said *ex tempore*, by one of his audience.

Every intelligent man regards Katterfelto as a windbag, in spite of his having such a crowd of followers. He has demonstrated to the people that the influenza originates from a sort of small insect which poisons the air. A quack remedy against this, which he claims to be successful, is eagerly bought up. For several days now he has advertised in the papers: 'Herr Katterfelto has, indeed, wanted rainy weather to kill the tiny pernicious insects in the air, but now he passionately desires nothing more than fine weather, because his Majesty and all the Royal Family have resolved that, come the first fine day, they will go to see with their own eyes the great wonder which this eminent scientist intends to demonstrate.'*

But the Royal Family have not yet even thought of see-

* Gustav Katterfelto (d. 1799). Came to London about 1782 and traded on widespread fear of the influenza epidemic then in being. He is referred to by Cowper in *The Task*. Moritz underestimated his power of persuasion, for the Royal Family saw his entertainment in 1784 and the King gave him a lavish testimonial.

ing Herr Katterfelto's wonder. This kind of bombast is very well dubbed in English as 'puff', which literally means a strong waft of wind and in a metaphorical sense means to brag or exaggerate.

The English papers are full of such 'puffs' every day – especially for quack ointments and medicines, by which means some have already become rich, including one of our nation who is known as 'the German Doctor'. An advertisement of a lottery reads thus: 'Ten thousand pounds for sixpence! Yes, astonishing as it may seem, it is nevertheless true that for a small stake of sixpence, ten thousand pounds and other main prizes to the value of £50,000 can be won! etc.'

But enough for the present about English windbags.

Yesterday I dined with Pastor Schrader, a son-in-law of Professor Forster of Halle. He is minister to St James's Chapel (having in addition a colleague and a reader, who although ordained, receives only fifty pounds a year). Pastor Schrader gives religious instruction to the young princes and princesses of the Royal Family. While visiting him I met the two chaplains who have been with the Hanoverian troops to Minorca – Herr Lindemann and Herr Kritter. They are now returned with the garrison. They were exposed to all the perils of the campaign. Like all civil servants in England, the German clergy have to pay a heavy tax out of their salaries.

The English clergy, especially in London, are notorious for their free and easy way of life. While I have been living here one of them has fought a duel in Hyde Park and shot his opponent. He was tried by jury and found guilty of manslaughter, or unpremeditated homicide, for which he was 'branded' on the hand with a cold iron, this being a privilege the nobility and clergy enjoy over other murderers.

Yesterday week after I had preached for Herr Wendeborn,

71

we found ourselves going by an English church where the sermon was still proceeding. We went in. A young man was preaching with the proper delivery and apparently good declamation but in the monotonous tone the English always affect. We went out of the church into the coffee-house opposite where we dined. It was not long before the preacher from across the way also entered. He asked for pen and ink, wrote several pages in a great hurry, as if they had just occurred to him, and stuck them in his pocket. Then he had dinner and immediately left the coffee-house and again entered the church opposite. We followed him. He went into the chancel, took his notes out of his pocket and delivered presumably the sermon he had prepared under our very eyes in the coffee-house.

In these coffee-houses quietness is the rule. If they speak, they speak softly together. Most of them read the papers and nobody disturbs another. The room is entered from the street directly by the front door and the seats are separated by wooden wainscotting. Many letters and proposals are written out: you can often see something in a newspaper dated from a coffee-house. So it is understandable that a clergyman can prepare a sermon there with the intention of delivering it immediately in a near-by church.

I have often taken another long walk, through Hanover Square and Cavendish Square to Bulstrode Street near Paddington, where the Danish Ambassador lives and where I have on several occasions visited Herr Schönborn, Secretary to the Danish Legation.* He is known in Germany for his experimental translation of Pindar and as a philosopher of fine intellect. I have spent some very pleasant hours with him. His life studies are empirical psychology and the philo-

* Gottlieb Friedrich von Schönborn (1737–1817): one of the group of men of letters gathered round the elder Bernstorff.

sophy of language. He has done excellent work in these subjects, the results of which I hope he will give to the world. His special subject is poetry – especially the Ode – and his knowledge cf Greek and Roman literature is profound. All he undertakes he does for the undertaking and not to seek fame. One might be tempted to say that it is a pity that so admirable a man is so retiring by nature, were it not that on reflection one sees this to have been generally characteristic of so many of the finest types of manhood in the past.

But what makes him estimable above all is his pure open mind and the excellence of his character, which have won him the love and trust of all his friends. He has already been Secretary to the Ambassador in Algiers, and now, here in England, he devotes himself to the study of philosophy whenever his official duties permit. The more agreeable his acquaintance with me the more difficult I shall find it to lose – as I soon must – the friendship and instructive conversation of this man.

I have seen the great Freemasons' Salon in the Freemasons' Tavern. This room is of astonishing height and breadth – almost like a church. The musicians' gallery is set high up and from it one can look down on the whole room, which makes a most majestic sight. It has been built at great cost, towards which the German lodges have contributed. Freemasonry is not, by the way, generally proscribed here because most of their assemblies are degenerated into drinking-clubs. Nevertheless I hope that there may be some masons who go to their lodge to unite in the high ideals vital to the Craft. The Duke of Cumberland is now Provincial Grand Master. *

* Duke of Cumberland, Henry Frederick (1745–90), son of Frederick, Prince of Wales, and brother of King George III, Grand Master of Grand Lodge of Freemasons from 1782.

SEVEN

Model for guide-books

London, June 20th, 1782

AT LAST MY DECISION to go into the country is to take effect. This afternoon I shall set out in the stage-coach, so this morning I am writing my last letter to you from London. That is, until I return from my wandering on foot, for as soon as I am out of the uncertain environs of London I shall no longer allow myself to be cooped up in a coach, but take my staff and strike out on foot. First, however, I will tell you of the things I have forgotten to write about previously, and what I have seen noteworthy in the past few days. Before all others:

ST PAUL'S CATHEDRAL

I must confess that on first entering this building its emptiness damped rather than stimulated the feeling of majesty I desired. All around me were huge empty walls and pillars, stone arches rose to an astonishing height above me and a smooth, flat marble pavement lay beneath me. There was no altar visible, nor indeed any sign to indicate that men assembled here to praise the Almighty; for the choir (or that part of the church where divine service is held) is screened off from the great round main structure by an iron gate. *

Consider on the other hand the temple of Nature. The blue arch of the heavens; the ground carpeted in green; a truly great temple. This is not void but filled with pointers to the presence of God. If men want to imitate this temple with their own handiwork, however, they must of necessity bring something into it to atone for the loss of the living bounty of Nature and reveal this as their aim. Of course, nobody can lay down the law on matters such as this, but it is well that someone should occasionally say what he thinks.

For a trifle of money I was shown over the church by a guide, whose rigmarole about how long it took to build, and all the rest of it, he delivered so mechanically that I wished he had kept it to himself. In the choir – separated as I have said from the main portion of the building by a screen – was the church proper, with benches and chairs, chancel and altar. At the sides were choir-stalls as in our cathedrals. This chapel seems to have been rightly built so that the Bishop or Dean need not strain his voice when preaching.

I was also taken to what is called the Whispering Gallery, which goes round the lower edge of the circumference of the astonishing cupola. I had to stand right opposite to my guide, at the other side of the gallery, so that the whole width of the church (or diameter of that huge circle) was between us. And as I stood there he slammed the door to, making a bang which sounded in my ears like a thunder-clap. Then I had to lay my ear to the wall, from which position I heard my guide's voice saying: 'Can you hear me?' spoken softly against the wall from the distance where he stood: but

* Ironwork by Jean Tijou.

sounding to me like a loud-clashing din. This amplification of sound at such a distance is truly wonderful; once in the *Ratskeller* at Bremen I heard something like it, but not to be compared for magnitude.

I then ascended another staircase to the great gallery which runs outside the dome, and there I remained nearly two hours, for so many are the surrounding objects of interest that the eye can never be satisfied. I wandered from side to side; from one direction to another, studying the view closely in order to impress upon my memory the unique picture before me. Beneath me lay a packed mass of towers, houses and palaces, with the London squares – their green lawns in their midst – adding pleasant splashes of colour in between.

At one end of the Thames stood the Tower of London, like a city with a forest of masts behind it; at the other lay Westminster Abbey lifting up its towers. The green hills skirting the Paddington and Islington districts smiled at me from afar off while nearer by lay Southwark on the opposite bank of the Thames. The city was almost too much to be taken in at a glance, extending as it did continuously in chains of houses by the sides of the highways as far as the places in the adjacent landscape.

How great had seemed Berlin to me when first I saw it from the tower of St Mary's and looked down on it from the hill at Tempelhof; how insignificant it now seemed when I set it in my imagination against London! It is vain to try to describe such a scene in words and even less in writing, for only a shadow of the impression can be so portrayed. He who would see a world in little, let him come here and gaze.

The roof of St Paul's itself, with its two small towers, lies beneath me now, looking like the hump of a low hill seen from a higher one. Gladly would I have remained longer, but a gust of wind – so strong at this height as to be hardly withstood – drove me down again.

Although St Paul's is very high in itself, its commanding presence is still further enhanced because the spot on which it is built is also high.

The *Petrikirche* in Berlin seems in spite of the difference of architectural style to have this resemblance to St Paul's in London, that at least it lifts up its great black roof in the same way above the surrounding buildings.

I saw also in St Paul's a wooden model of itself, said to have been made before the church was built.* It may be compared interestingly with the huge building.

St Paul's Churchyard is surrounded by an iron railing which seems very lengthy if you have to walk it. The site however is not by any means spacious, for this superb church is well-nigh built-about by houses. A marble statue of Queen Anne serves to grace the enclosed space before the church. Also the great bell of St Paul's is noteworthy, being reckoned one of the largest in Europe. I believe it should rank after that in Vienna.

Everything I saw in St Paul's cost me no more than a little over a shilling, paid out bit by bit in pennies and half-pennies as determined by the set fees payable for the privilege of seeing the various things of interest.

WESTMINSTER ABBEY

I saw Westminster Abbey on a dark and melancholy day, in keeping with the character of the place.

I went in through the small door that leads straight into the Poets' Corner where memorials to the foremost poets, authors and artists are placed.

* Wren's 'Great Model' which stood on the site while the cathedral was being built. It can still be seen in St Paul's.

Immediately on entering I saw the statue of Shakespeare not far from the door, dressed in the costume of his day, with a collar round his throat, and so on. Near by stands Garrick's memorial. A passage from *The Tempest* describing solemnly, peacefully, the end of all things, most aptly graces its creator's monument.

Rowe's memorial is not far off, placed near his beloved Shakespeare, as the inscription tells us, at his own wish. I saw the bust of Goldsmith also in the same company. Like Butler (whose memorial is a little farther on), he had hardly enough bread in his lifetime and now after death he has been given a stone.

The memorials of Milton, Dryden, Gay and Thomson stand almost in a row. Gay's has a very touching inscription said to have been written by himself:

> Life is a jest and all things show it:
> I thought so once and now I know it.

Our German Händel has his life-size monument here, and there are others honouring the actress Miss Pritchard and the actor Booth.

Newton's memory is upheld by a splendid memorial in the choir, over the entrance, with another right opposite, below in the church, drawing attention to the first one.

As I went along the side walls of the Abbey I saw that they were devoted almost entirely to monuments to great admirals carved in marble, which make but a pointless impression with all their pomp and embellishment. I came back always with the greatest pleasure to the Poets' Corner, to see again those superb heads of years ago now in confident companionship together. In particular the tasteful simplicity of the sculpture lent an air of repose to my mind, bringing to remembrance some favourite passage from the works of Shakespeare or Milton, and with it something of the spirit of those great dead.

I found no memorial there to Addison or Pope. The graves of the kings, and a few other noteworthy sights in Westminster Abbey I have not seen. Possibly I may see these when I am back in London after my trip in the country.

I have now made all my preparations for this journey. I have an accurate map of England in my pocket, together with an excellent guide-book lent to me by Mr Pointer, the English merchant to whom I was recommended from Hamburg, and entitled: *A New and accurate Description of all the direct and principal Cross-roads in Great Britain.* This book I hope will serve me well in my wanderings.

For a long time I was uncertain which direction to take – whether to go to the Isle of Wight, to Portsmouth Harbour, or to Derbyshire which is renowned for its natural curiosities and its romantic scenery. I have chosen this last place. I shall leave my travelling-chest with Mr Pointer during my absence so that I shall not have to pay for lodgings without occupying them. Mr Pointer has been a long time in Germany; he likes us and speaks good German; he is a very courteous and likeable man, intelligent and with good taste. I was recommended to him by Herr Persent and Herr Dörner in Hamburg, to whom I had been introduced by Herr Geheimrat von Tauberheim in Berlin. I am sure this recommendation will stand me in good stead.

Today I shall travel as far as Richmond. The stage-coach starts at two o'clock from a spot near Newchurch in the Strand. I shall take with me only four guineas, some spare linen, my guide-book, map and pocket-book, as well as

Milton's *Paradise Lost* which I have stuck in my pocket, and I hope to travel very lightly with just these.

Well! It has already struck half-past one and is time I was at the coach. Farewell! I shall write to you again from Richmond.

Interlude

MORITZ'S
ENGLAND

★

Moritz's England

I

CARL PHILIP MORITZ loved his native land; his life's ambition was to serve the German people, but as he looked out from the ship bearing him up the Thames Estuary he saw a land which, he said, surpassed his own as the spring surpasses autumn. He saw a river teeming with trading ships and beyond them a landscape rich and beautiful. A lucky island!

He saw the novelty of a landscape divided up by growing hedges, with here and there wooded copses; the country seats of the gentry stood out in their superior environment of green parks, the towns were neat, villages nestled in the places where they had grown up.

All this was very different from Frederick the Great's Berlin, but it was not unexpected to a man like Moritz, for he had read some English literature and from the new novels of that time he had got an inkling of the characters of squire, parson, farmers and their womenfolk. He was to see all these on his travels through England; and he accurately described them, for Moritz was an observant man writing to a friend as well read as himself.

In Berlin there were soldiers in every street and the state was ruled by an aristocracy which was a closed caste. The English aristocracy was rather different: only the eldest sons of the family took the titles and land; the younger sons made their own way in the world – at sea, in the army, the church, the law or in commerce. They were not cut off socially from their brothers whose lot it was to carry on the family estates. The landowners got themselves elected to parliament or sat in the House of Lords, but everyone with sufficient standing had a vote – Moritz saw how it worked at an election – and could cast it whichever way he thought his interests lay.

It would be idle to pretend that Moritz did not know there might be corruption, but he found a great deal of evidence to show how men tried to expose it. He was shocked at the personal abuse thrown about in the House of Commons and at the open accusations made in the Press. He held in contempt the way that politicians and actors had to appease the mob, but he gave that mob credit for a taste in good oratory and he found that great numbers of the humbler people knew their English literature. He even found a saddler who quoted Latin authors. He saw the decoy ship near Tower Hill, set there to serve the evil purpose of the press-gang, but he heard his landlady's small son say 'I will shed every drop of my blood for my country' – voluntarily! And one day the boy came in with a broadside ballad, evidently a version of the story of Admiral Benbow:

Brave Benbow lost his legs by chain-shot, by chain-shot;
Brave Benbow lost his legs by chain-shot.
   Brave Benbow lost his legs,
   And on his stumps he begs:
'Fight on, my English lads, 'tis our lot, 'tis our lot!'

This type of ballad represented a kind of faith among the common English people even though they knew the horrors of life at sea. It is one of the irrational forces – Methodism was another – which kept the English loyal when the French turned to revolution. Another was the belief that they could pull themselves out of the mess they were in by making just laws. Moritz saw the process in the House of Commons.

For the most part we can leave Moritz's pages to speak for themselves, but in the matter of politics this would be difficult. The situation was confused. Lord North's government had fallen shortly before Moritz arrived in England, and his first visits were made as the Whig government under Lord Rockingham, with Fox and Shelburne sharing the main responsibilities under him, was trying to cope with the situation. Moritz's later visit, after his return from Derbyshire, saw this government split, for Rockingham died suddenly on July 1st, 1782, and a new government had to be created. Let us then take a look at the characters Moritz mentions.

We can conveniently start with Richard Rigby (1722–1788), whom Moritz heard carping about the possibility that Lord Rodney's pension might be cut if it were known that he had taken any considerable prizes of war. Of course Rodney had taken prizes. He had won a great naval victory and put the Spanish fleet out of action for a long time, besides capturing some five thousand Spanish soldiers. But he had allowed some of the Spanish ships to escape, greatly to the disgust of some of his captains – especially Hood, for a threat to the supply-line to the American Colonies thus remained. Parliament had thereupon sent out Admiral Pigot to take over Rodney's command. Later they learned more of the battle and sent an express to stop Pigot, but too late. Admiral Rodney was in England now awaiting the decision of a parliament that had something of a guilty conscience. He was elevated to the peerage and awarded a pension of two thousand pounds a year, but not given a further command. Fox had been responsible for Admiral Rodney's recall, and, as Moritz observed, had lost some popular favour in consequence; he was fighting to get it back.

Rigby had been an oppressor of Wilkes, mostly by means of bogus petitions, and had opposed Greville's Bribery Act in 1769 on the ground that it would stop treating at election times. His parliamentary life is a story of corruption which he evidently regarded as natural to the situation. General Conway once said of Dundas and Rigby that they had 'the gift of tongues – double tongues!' He was urging the renunciation of attempts to reduce America by force.

This loss of thirteen valuable colonies rankled in the minds of all. Britain's humiliation was complete: she had been defeated in arms and had failed in diplomacy. The government of King's Friends under Lord North had collapsed and the Whigs under Rockingham were struggling against the enmity of George III, who was still able to buy support with royal patronage. Fox was insistent on his claim that he acted as a free man in supporting Sir Cecil Wray at the Westminster election; he wanted above all to make clear that he had made no secret bargain with the King on being made Secretary of State. Such bargains were made.

Sir Cecil Wray was a wealthy landowner with a will of his own where his tenants were concerned – in fact something of a tyrant. He had the support of Fox at his election in 1782 – the election which Moritz attended – but in the famous election of 1784 he fought against Fox. Wray had always been a strong opponent of the American war, not for reasons of convenience but belief. Financially and intellectually Wray was independent. When Fox later threw in his lot with Lord North in the infamous coalition of 1783, Wray broke away. It was at this 1784 election that the Duchess of Devonshire canvassed votes for Fox with kisses, and the event is commemorated to this day by the inn-sign of *The Intrepid Fox* in Soho. The landlord of this tavern, Samuel House, changed his sign as part of his campaign on behalf of Fox, and there the most prominent of Whig politicians could be found at that time.

Nobody's hands were quite clean in English politics and one can sympathize with the American colonists when they saw no hope of justice from that quarter even though their part was being taken by several able members of parliament. The parliament we see is guided by men striving to put their house in order. Rockingham's short government carried through a few reforms but had not enough time to complete its work. The King was eccentric but clever; on the death of Rockingham he put Shelburne in office and Fox got out. That is the situation we find when Moritz returned to London and again visited the House of Commons. Fox, Burke and Lord John Cavendish had resigned, and Shelburne replaced Cavendish by the young William Pitt as Chancellor of the Exchequer.

Burke, whose policies had guided the Rockingham ministry, was an established and able member. Moritz's description of him is very apt — quelling with a glance and a single scathing reference to his seniority the chattering of the backbenchers. There is another account of his speech, differing from Moritz's in that he referred not to the fable of the wolf and the lamb but to Little Red Riding-hood who 'didn't know a wolf from her grandmother'. Anyway, General Conway was defending the government from attacks by Fox, whose personal dislike of Shelburne was partly his, Fox's, reason for resigning. There was the other reason, too, that

Fox wanted the independence of America to be uncondi-
tional, while Shelburne wanted to make it a condition of
peace. The end of this government was almost in sight at its
formation, but we must thank Moritz for that independent
view of the young Mr Pitt.

They bickered and plotted, changed sides and looked
after themselves. But in the process they were involved in
great events and they were thrown willy-nilly into the discussion of mighty issues. Moral principles had to be espoused
and defended, and advantage taken of any expediency to get
them passed. Some of these men were great by nature while
others had some measure of greatness thrust upon them by
the terrific tension of the times. India, Gibraltar, America
and Ireland were discussed across the floor of the House, and
these were historic matters. Moritz does not seem to have
understood all, but he saw the English gentry at one of their
tasks.

They thought it no harm to be making money in pro-
fessions devoted to the public good. Mr Green kept a boarding-school admittedly for profit, and evidently organized
each moment of the boys' time for their improvement much
as a time-and-motion specialist deals today with factory per-
sonnel. Mr Modd the Oxford don was doing a brisk trade in
delivering sermons for those who could not preach, and there
is a slanderous reference at the end of the book to a Jew in
London writing sermons for all comers. But Moritz was
deeply touched by the sincerity of a village church service
at Nettlebed, even though the parson was a bit of a snob. He
seems to have missed entirely the most vital religious force
of the time, however – the Methodists.

Only from the pulpits does Moritz admit to hearing bad
oratory. He strongly advised anyone wishing to acquire good
English declamation to visit the theatres, despite the atro-

cious behaviour of their audiences. David Garrick was dead; Moritz saw no actor of Garrick's standard. The theatre he visited could only perform legitimate drama when the major theatres – Drury Lane and Covent Garden – were closed. This concession had been wrung from the King through the mediation of his brother the Duke of York, by Samuel Foote, whose play *The Nabob* Moritz has described. Foote's ambition was to play good drama in his theatre in the Haymarket, but this he was forbidden to do; for Charles II had granted patents to the theatres of Drury Lane and Covent Garden which gave them a monopoly of legitimate drama. Foote used subterfuges like inviting an audience to see a rehearsal which was in fact a proper performance, and charging them half-a-crown for a cup of chocolate, but all to no avail.

Success came by the back door. Foote was an incorrigible boaster and claimed among other things, at a party at Lord Mexborough's seat, Methley Park, near Leeds, that he could ride any horse in his lordship's stables. They took him at his word and found him one which threw him. Foote broke a leg; only an amputation saved his life. The joke had thus gone too far, so the Duke of York (for whose delight the trick had mainly been played) visited Foote in his sick-room and asked if there was anything he could do to help. He probably expected Foote to ask for money. If so, he had overlooked Foote's ambition to be able to produce Shakespearian drama in London without let or hindrance. Foote asked for a dramatic licence for the Haymarket Theatre.

This was granted only for the summer months, when the two other patent theatres were closed, so that Foote (as he himself used to say) got only one foot in the theatre. The successor to this theatre is still called the Theatre Royal, Haymarket.

The goings-on in 1782 would be just as Moritz described

them. He did not, however, see the main attraction of the season, which was *The Beggar's Opera*, by John Gay, first produced in 1728 as a counterblast to the artificial entertainment of baroque opera then in vogue. Gay's beggar proclaimed his opera to be 'true to Nature' and in so doing started a hare which Moritz himself was very busily chasing. All Moritz's appraisement of art is based on its realistic delineation of human emotions – whether in Vauxhall Gardens or All Souls College, Oxford. He saw St Paul's Cathedral as splendidly empty of the spirit of the Great Architect (a term which as a German Freemason he might well have used), but the actual work of God in Nature, as he saw it in the Great Peak Cavern, moved him to pray. In *The Beggar's Opera* Gay showed the criminal classes much as these were explained to Moritz by a travelling companion, but Gay did more: he inspired a young artist named Hogarth to break away from the baroque influence of his fashionable father-in-law Sir James Thornhill (whose paintings in St Paul's and All Souls College Moritz must have seen but does not mention), and Hogarth's prints were to be found in inns about the country, as Moritz says. Another young man to be influenced was Fielding the novelist – the admission is in the Preface to *Joseph Andrews* – and yet Moritz missed seeing Gay's play although he saw his tomb. Was Moritz the unsuccessful actor too respectable?

We cannot of course blame Moritz for not seeing everything; the wonder is that he saw so much in so short a time. Like all of us, he failed to mention those things in which he was not particularly interested. He tells us about the theatre but mentions none of the singers at Vauxhall Gardens or Ranelagh by name. Did he hear 'The Lass of Richmond Hill' sung at Vauxhall? It was composed by Dr James Hook, permanent organist at Vauxhall Gardens about the time when Moritz visited England. That is the sort of music he would hear there and would probably remember when he saw Richmond Hill for himself; and who are we to turn sour on him and say that Leonard McNally, who wrote the lyric of this delightful song, had Richmond, Yorkshire, in mind? Richmond, Surrey, has every virtue Moritz saw in it.

II

From the first day that Moritz began to tramp the roads of England a theme runs through his commentary: *a pedestrian is held in contempt in this land of plenty*. When he asked the officer with whom he travelled in the coach why the English did not sometimes take a walk themselves, he was satisfied with the answer: 'They are too rich and too lazy.'

This is too glib an answer, if only because others found difficulties on the road when travelling by coach. The roads were being far more used than previously and innkeepers had no lack of guests. Some were mercenary and took all they could get for as little as they could give, but these were the exception. There was a tradition of good innkeeping on the main roads and, no matter what complaints there may have been of some inns, the general standard was improving. Moreover, there were the county hotels with their assembly rooms – centres of local society; these were growing in number. They did not want a low type of guest.

But there were others. Let us turn for a moment to the song-writer Charles Dibdin, who made many journeys about the country in the course of his profession. The first of these he undertook in 1787–8 and published an account of it in the latter year. Like Moritz he carried in his pocket Daniel Patterson's *Description of all the direct and principal Cross-roads in Great Britain* which was to the coaching age what the A.A. Handbook is to ours, and like an A.A. route-chart it mentioned the places to be seen on the way. Dibdin went to many of the places visited by Moritz and we can compare their remarks. Let us then read Dibdin on inns; here he is at the White Lion in Stratford-upon-Avon:

> Common justice obliges me to say that the insolence of the people who keep it exceeds all example. I pass by the insolence with which they treat travellers in a stage coach (which is hard, by the way, for they must go there or nowhere) and also their wanting to put me in a return chaise and make me pay the full price for it: all this is in the way of business. But, when you are in a hurry, to have the very worst horses picked out, and be told 'the others are for your betters, and you may have these or none', though they do not know you (and if they did, your betters do not pay a farthing more) is a species of contemptuous impudence that I hope will be taken down by someone more competent than me.
>
> I have a great deal more of this sort of conduct to complain of, and I shall seriously advise all respectable inhabitants of capital towns (for at Stratford I know not if it would be worth while) for their own private bene-fit, for the benefit of those who in business visits pam-per the pride and fatten these insufferable innkeepers, and for the benefit of the public in general, to imitate the spirit of the Duke of Norfolk and as completely curb the impertinence of these servants out of livery (which in general they are).

By his last sentence Dibdin implies that many inn-keepers and their waiters, chambermaids and the like, had been in the domestic service of the gentry and felt it beneath their dignity to bow and scrape to common people. Bowing and scraping was the custom at an inn, as Moritz noted when the post-chaise drew up at The Bull in Nettlebed.

Dibdin was on his way from Oxford to Birmingham, so it seems likely that the White Lion was the inn at which Moritz also changed horses. The Duke of Norfolk to whom he refers was a renowned trencherman and has been credited with the introduction of late dining. The meal to which Moritz refers as dinner was eaten in the middle of the day; the evening meal was supper.

We can move farther up the social scale and still find travellers who were treated rudely. Lord Torrington stayed at the same inn and complained in his diary that they gave him a dog-hole of a room, froze him, and the very dog turned up its nose at the veal cutlets they set out for his dinner, whereupon he would willingly have kicked the cook. His horse was not properly bedded, neither was Lord Torrington. He stopped sixpence off the bill. Yet on two previous occasions he had had no cause for complaint.

The roads on which they travelled were made of local stone with a high crown to enable the water to run off. This it did, but drainage from there was according to the accidents of geography. Moreover, having so high a crown, vehicles were not safe on the sides of the road, so they drove in the middle and soon there were two deep ruts where the wheels ran; roadmending consisted in filling up these holes when labour was available. These were the improved turnpike roads, maintained by trusts acting under authority given to them by parliament and paid for by travellers at the turnpike gates. Freehold of the roads was not vested in the turnpike trusts, which were in theory temporary, ready to go out of business when they had put the roads in order and recovered their costs. Apart from the turnpike roads, all other roads were the responsibility of the parish and in theory had to be repaired by the parishioners themselves, each of whom could be called on to give six days' free labour on the roads each year. A local official called the waywarden was expected to get them to do it! The obligation to work six days on the roads persisted until 1835, when it was swept away together with other out-of-date regulations. Moritz used local roads in the Derbyshire Peak, but elsewhere he used the turnpike roads. The coaches were as he described them, with outside passengers hanging on as best they could, but soon seats outside were provided front and back. It is still possible to travel from The Mitre in Oxford to Woodstock in or on a stage-coach (along the road which Moritz travelled in a coach), and The Mitre is still one of the finest inns in England, serving town and gown as characteristically as in Moritz's day.

Oxford dons do not, however, behave in The Mitre as Moritz saw them doing; reform has raised its ugly head in Oxford time and time again and all that is left to them is the mild eccentricity of resisting all reform. Their main frustration nowadays is road traffic. They still talk of the High as the finest street in Europe, and Cambridge men still show them their Backs. The Fellows of All Souls had a way with them in the nineteen thirties which brought them under grave suspicion of sympathy with dictatorship, but that has passed, as indeed have former little foibles. In Moritz's time this College was like a private club – almost a family club – and among other interests they were caught using the University Press to print obscene publications.

The fact that they were caught and stopped from going on with it shows that there was still some discipline in Oxford. Mr Modd was Chaplain of Corpus Christi College and on one occasion he was admonished for drunkenness. But in a society where men held sinecures and were at the same time sworn to celibacy, certain sins grew like rank weeds – drinking, wenching and currying favour from the rich. Dibdin was particularly trenchant:

> The young gentlemen of the University have generally separate tutors. I do not say the following remarks apply to every tutor, but do they (the tutors), [as] generally understood, consider anything but the pleasures of the pupil? Nay, are they not often commanded to do so? Are not his wishes anticipated? Is there an incentive to idleness, a stimulative to dissipation, but what it is their study to procure? Are misdemeanours to be investigated? They wrack invention to find an excuse! Is pleasure the word? The tutor is the jolliest fellow in the throng!
>
> In short – would you teach your son to trample upon reason, violate decorum, destroy every social trace of virtue ... and knock down order, give him a tutor that will pass muster among the rest. If he be of any other description he will be hunted down with undeserved calumny till he shall be obliged, either to take refuge in a school, or behind the reading-desk of a country curate.

Like Mr Green's usher, in fact, whom Moritz saw in Paddington. Yet a young man could work in the university if he were determined. Charles James Fox studied so hard that the head of his college advised him to desist, and Fox was as profligate as any undergraduate Dibdin could have had in mind. Samuel Johnson spent but four terms at Oxford, poor and bitter, with little respect for his tutor, but he loved the place in later life. There is indeed something very powerful in the personality of Oxford University, like a mistress you cannot wholly do without.

All the dons were ordained clergymen and so long as they kept their orthodoxy they were safe. Mr Modd's strictures on Dr Joseph Priestley* were in accordance with the general behaviour of his colleagues. Meanwhile Dr Priestley lived in a non-corporate town – Birmingham – where he just evaded the law against dissenters. There he remained while the mob, shouting 'Church and King', burnt down his house and chapel in 1791. They also shouted 'Down with all philosophers', by which they could have meant scientists (for Priestley discovered a way to produce oxygen) or thinkers such as Moritz himself, whose views by 1791 had led them to support in principle the French Revolution. It is a pity that Moritz got out of Birmingham so quickly and passed through Lichfield without further inquiries. But how was he to know that in these centres were intellectuals whom he would dearly have enjoyed meeting: the men of the new scientific age, based on reason and the laws of nature? In the Lunar Club in Lichfield there used to meet Matthew Boulton the great ironfounder of Birmingham and his associates, James Watt and William Murdoch, Josiah Wedgwood the great potter, Thomas Day, author of *Sandford and Merton*, Miss Anna Sewell, 'the Swan of Lichfield' whose opinion on literature was law, and Dr Erasmus Darwin, who sang the praises of the new industrial achievements in formal couplets:

So with strong arm immortal Brindley leads
His long canals and parts the velvet meads.
Winding in lucid lanes, the watery mass
Minds the firm rock, or loads the deep morass;
While rising locks a thousand hills alarm,
Flings o'er a thousand streams his silver arm;
Feeds the long vales, the nodding woodland laves,
And plenty, arts and commerce freight the waves.

* See pp. 126–7.

It is a mere commonplace of history, this going out of skilled handicrafts before the onrush of machinery, yet do we want things to be as they were? What sort of life had the guide who conducted Moritz through the Castleton cave? The shoemaker in Castleton complained of the poor living, although Moritz says he was an excellent craftsman; and the saddler from Tideswell, son of a man of means, had to go to Matlock to obtain work – and walk home. There is much to be learnt from Moritz's evidence even when he makes no comment on it himself. What was it about the scene between Bakewell and Ashford that so reminded him of his boyhood home in Germany? It would seem that he had arrived at a part of England where the agricultural improvements of the eighteenth century had not yet been applied, and the land was being farmed on the old open-strip system:

> Little Boy Blue, come, blow your horn;
> The sheep's in the meadow, the cow's in the corn.

Enclosures had put little boy blues out of work, and their parents, if they lacked the capital needed for the new methods, lost their rights to the common land and became employees of the new landowners. Some writers were shocked; among them Moritz's idol Oliver Goldsmith:

> Ill fares the land, to hast'ning ills a prey,
> Where wealth accumulates and men decay;
> Princes and lords may flourish or may fade;
> A breath can make them as a breath has made;
> But a bold peasantry, their country's pride,
> When once destroy'd can never be supplied.

What happened to a man who lost his common rights to the land and could find no employment? By the great Poor Law of Elizabeth he had to be kept by his parish. But this was a disgraceful situation; he incurred the contempt of his neighbours. As likely as not he would try his luck elsewhere. Then he would become a 'poor travelling creature' as one woman described Moritz to his disgust, and if he tried to settle in any parish they would drive him out for fear he should become dependent on them. It was the duty of the village constable to whip vagrants from the parish – men or women. Apart from that, there is a conservative feeling among those who live in small communities; they do not like strangers to this day, and in the old days they did not always want a stranger to find out what went on in their peaceful village.

Moritz seems not to have known about the provisions of the Poor Law, but those who warned him not to go about on foot did so with good intentions. He must have been mistaken for a vagrant in Burton, for example; one cannot think otherwise why he was hissed at. The Harcourt Arms at Nuneham Courtney, where he was scurvily treated, is a good inn, and was in Moritz's time, but it served as a place of rest for those having business at the Big House, and Lord Harcourt owned and controlled the whole village. The Bull's Head at Wardlow, where the landlady had difficulty with the account, is still much as Moritz described it. The present landlady looks after the inn while her husband is out at work and they keep some livestock – one cow, one pig, some hens and turkeys – serve good beer and offer accommodation at fifteen shillings and sixpence for bed and breakfast or eighteen shillings and sixpence for the same with dinner, or did when last I was there (1961). Only a fool would walk the main roads now, for what were busy in Moritz's day are now practically traffic-bound, but you can go from Richmond along the Thames towpath to Henley, taking your time, go over the Chilterns from Henley to

Nettlebed by several paths or along a pleasant-enough road. You can turn off the Oxford road at Dorchester to climb Sinodun and see the ancient earthworks there, and if you have to go all the rest of the way to Matlock by vehicle, the High Peak is a walkers' paradise and a National Park. The Great Peak Cavern is only one of several to be seen at Castleton,* and London still offers many of the attractions Moritz saw.

Canaletto's paintings of London will bring to you the scenes that Moritz loved, and Sir Joshua Reynolds lived in one of the houses Moritz so admired on Richmond Terrace. From his window he painted the scene which Moritz got up early in the morning to see. It is now in the Tate Gallery. There are Ackerman's views of Oxford and Rowlandson's cartoons of Oxford life. All these are part of Moritz's England, but most valuable of all are the intimate portraits he himself has left us: Little Jacky and his mother, the footpad near Maidenhead, Mr Modd, the female chimney-sweep at Sutton Coldfield, the erudite saddler, the cobbler of Castleton, the adventures of the Devil's Cavern, midnight in The Mitre, riding in the luggage-boot of a coach and, above all, that incomparable Sunday morning at Nettlebed. The English are the richer for Moritz's observation.

* The lead mine Moritz mentions is now shown to visitors as the Speedwell Cavern.

Part Two

ON TOUR

*

EIGHT

Richmond:
the perfect town

So AT NOON yesterday I travelled for the first time in a stage-coach. These coaches are very elegant; they are lined inside and fitted with two seats, each of which is intended for three people, although I admit that when the full number is carried they are a bit packed.

But only an elderly lady got in with me at the starting-point at the White Hart. As we rolled along farther, however, the coach filled up – mostly with females. These women hardly knew one another and their interchange of gossip was rather trite and long-winded. I took out my guide-book and read about the road we were taking.

Before you realize you have left London you are already in Kensington, Hammersmith and so on, for the unbroken line of houses stretches on interminably down both sides of the street even after you have left the town, just as when going from Berlin to Schöneberg, although the appearance of the scenery, the houses and streets is of course very different.

It was a beautiful day and I should have dearly enjoyed

more time to admire the exquisite outlook on both sides, but our coach rolled inconsiderately on. Not far out of London I noticed an exceptionally fine white house in the distance, and by the roadside where we drove, a signpost told us in unmistakable wording that this magnificent white mansion was in fact a boarding-school!

The man who sat beside me pointed out to us the various seats of the nobility and gentry as we passed them by, and entertained us with lurid tales of highway robberies committed in this area, so that the womenfolk began to be a bit alarmed. Then he began to stand up for the honour of English highwaymen against the dishonour of the French. The English, he said, robbed you, but the French robbed you and murdered you as well. Nevertheless, he went on, there is in England a sort of low rogue who murders too, and often for the merest trifle he may plunder from the body. These rogues are called footpads and are the lowest class of English criminals.

For English rogues may conveniently be divided into three grades:

The cream of criminal society are the pickpockets, who are to be found everywhere – even in the best company – often clean and well-dressed, so that they may be mistaken for people of some standing. In fact they may actually be so, for there are men who have fallen into want by reason of extravagance and are reduced to this way of living.

After them in order of rank come the highwaymen, who ride on horseback and often, in their desire to relieve the traveller of his purse, put him in terror with an unloaded pistol. But such men have been known to return part of their plunder to a victim gravely distressed, and in any event they do not murder lightly.

Then comes the third, the lowest and vilest class of

criminal – the footpads. Tragic examples may be read almost daily in English newspapers of poor people met on the road who have been brutally murdered for a few shillings. These thieves probably murder because they are unable to take flight like the highwayman on his horse, and so, should anyone live to give information concerning them, they can be pretty easily overtaken by a hue-and-cry.

But to get back to our stage-coach. I must not forget that there is another way of travelling – not in, but on, the vehicle. Poor people who cannot afford to pay much ride in this way – on the top of the coach without any seat or handhold being provided. They sit there anyhow they can, with their legs dangling over the side.

This is called 'riding on the outside', for which they are charged only half as much as those who ride 'on the inside'. We had another six passengers over our heads in this way and they made a terrific clatter with their frequent mounting and dismounting.

If you can keep a level balance on the top of a coach you can sit there well enough, and in some ways you should be better off than those riding inside, especially on a hot day, and the view of the surrounding scenery is better, but the companionship is a trifle plebeian and the dust a nuisance. Those riding inside can at least shut the windows.

In Kensington, where we pulled up, a Jew wanted to join us; but there was no room inside and he didn't want to ride on the outside. This caused my travelling companions to demur. They couldn't understand why a Jew should be ashamed of travelling on the outside; anyway, as they said, he was nothing but a Jew! I have noticed that here in England this anti-Semitic prejudice is far stronger than it is among us Germans.

I could catch only interrupted glimpses of the great

country houses and charming villas we passed, by peering sideways through the windows of the coach, which made me wish to be soon out of this rolling prison.

Towards evening we arrived at Richmond. I had paid a shilling before leaving London and here in Richmond I paid another; so my drive from London to Richmond cost me only two shillings.

As soon as I had stepped into an inn and had ordered supper, I went out to see the town and its environment.

I could see at once that the town was more removed, pleasanter and brighter than London. The houses were not so begrimed with smoke. The people also seemed to be more companionable; they sat on benches in front of their houses enjoying the cool evening air. A group of boys with some young men among them were playing ball on a beautiful green lawn in the middle of the town. In the streets a rural peace reigned, at any rate as compared with London, and I breathed a cleaner and a fresher air.

Then I went out of the town, over a bridge across the Thames at which you have to pay a penny toll each time you pass. The bridge is built in a graceful, lofty curve and leads straight into a charming valley along the bank of the Thames.

It was evening. The sun sent its last low rays along the valley. But this evening and this valley I shall never forget! In its way it was the purest revelation of Nature that I have ever seen in my life. What she vouchsafed to me in that moment no pen of man can describe. How I rued now every hour that I had delayed in London! I reproached a thousand times the irresolution that had kept me for so long in a gross prison when all the time I could have lingered in this paradise!

Yes. Whatever picture of paradise your imagination

paints, you will find the subject-matter of it here in this exquisite place. Here Thomson and Pope surely collected the charming sketches from which their inimitable paintings of Nature were assembled.

Instead of the wild clamour in and around London, I saw in the distance a few families walking hand-in-hand by the bank of the Thames. There breathed a soft calm here that opened up my heart to pure delight.

Under my feet sprang the springy turf which only grows on English ground; on one side of me a wood such as Nature could not create more beautiful; on the other the Thames with its shelving bank that rises like an amphitheatre, and a glimpse of high white houses seen through the dark green of trees that lie shimmering in the valley.

O Richmond! Richmond! Never shall I forget the evening when you smiled on me from your soft round hills and eased my mind of all its cares as I moved enraptured in your flowery river-meads!

Happy am I to be so seasonably freed from within those melancholy walls.

Oh, how you have bewitched me with your fresh-flowering complexion, the green pastures and broad streams of this most fortunate land! Let me not be withheld from returning to those barren, sand-blown plains which destiny has cast to be the scene of my activity; only let the memory of this scene go with me to assure me brighter hours in the trial that is to come.

So thought I, my good friend, on my lonely walk; and indeed yesterday evening was one of the choicest of my life.

I made a firm resolve to set out early in the morning and take that walk again. Now, thought I, I have seen this treasure only in the dim light of the moon, but think how it will shine in the light of morn!

Only, this hope was unfulfilled.

It is a general rule that if a man would preserve a great delight he should prepare himself against some trivial vexation. So it was with me here. I had dallied somewhat late and when I turned to go back to Richmond I found I had forgotten the name of the inn from which I had set out. I found the place with difficulty after having wandered through pretty well the whole town.

When I arrived I told them all about my walk and they, for their part, extolled the beauty of the view from Richmond Hill, which was that very same on which I had seen the white houses shimmering from the valley. I resolved that I would see the sunrise from this hill the following morning.

I was late getting to sleep, however, because of the noise of the hostess scolding her servants in the night. Nevertheless I was up again at three o'clock in the morning, only to appreciate Missbrauch's criticism of living in a country like England where they all get up so late; for, since nobody was awake, I could not get out of the house. I had to wait three seemingly interminable hours before I could be released.

The house-boy finally opened the door at six o'clock and I was soon ascending Richmond Hill. But consider my annoyance: the sky was overcast — had been so for an hour — and was now grown so cloudy that I could not enjoy one-half the exquisite prospect I knew must be there.

On top of the hill is an avenue of chestnut trees beneath which are placed some seats, distributed here and there. Behind this avenue stands a row of remarkably beautiful country houses, in an ideal situation if only because of the purity of the air you breathe there.

All the way down to the Thames the side of the hill was clothed in growing greenery. The Thames itself flows round in nearly half a circle, embracing wooded plains dotted with meadows and stately houses. On one side of the hill the town with its high bridge can be seen, on the other the sombre woodlands.

In the distance appeared little villages against a background of meadows and woods, so this outlook remains one of the finest I have seen in my life, despite the troubled weather.

But why is it that yesterday my imagination was more lively, my impressions far stronger and more romantic as I gazed up at the hill from the valley, than they were this morning, when I saw for myself this valley from the hill and knew what was actually there?

Now I have finished my breakfast, gripped my staff and am about to set out on foot. You will hear from me again from Windsor.

NINE

Eton and Windsor

NOW, MY FRIEND, writing to you from here, I have already undergone so many hardships as a pedestrian that I am undecided whether to continue in this manner or not.

A pedestrian seems in this country to be a sort of beast of passage – stared at, pitied, suspected and shunned by everybody who meets him. So at least it has proved on my way from Richmond to Windsor.

My host at Richmond was greatly astonished at my declared intention to walk to Oxford, and even beyond; but he nevertheless sent his small son with me to put me on to the right road for Windsor.

At first I went along a very pleasant footpath by the side of the Thames, the Royal Garden lying on my right; on the opposite side of the river lay Isleworth, a spot distinguished by several fine houses and gardens. Here I was ferried across

* This date is an error. If Moritz left London on June 20th he would be writing from Windsor on the 22nd.

the river to reach the Oxford road, which passes through Windsor.

As soon as I was on the other side I went to a house and asked a man standing at the door if I was on the right road for Oxford.

'Yes,' he said, 'but you'll want a carriage to get you there.'

I answered that I intended to go there on foot, whereupon he gave me a look full of meaning, shook his head and went in the house.

I was now on a very fine, broad road, with many vehicles of all sorts. It was a hot day, so these sent up a heavy cloud of dust. As usual in this country, however, the highway was bordered by those lovely green hedges which contribute so greatly to its attraction, and when I was tired I would sit down occasionally in the shade of one of them and read my Milton. But it was soon evident to me that travellers riding and driving by all regarded me with surprise and made that same significant gesture, as if they took me to be someone not quite sane. So must anyone seem, apparently, who sits by a public road reading a book. I soon saw that if I wanted to rest and read I must find some lonely spot in a by-lane.

As I went on again every passing coachman called out to me: 'Do you want to ride on the outside?' If I met only a farm worker on a horse he would say to me companionably: 'Warm walking, sir', and when I passed through a village the old women in their bewilderment would let out a 'God Almighty!'

The road was very pleasant as far as Hounslow. Beyond, it was somewhat unsatisfactory, going over a pretty wide heath – yet I saw sheep grazing here and there.

I was now growing somewhat tired, when I found to my surprise that, for once, a tree standing alone in the midst of the heath had been fitted with a seat around its base, beneath the graceful leafy shade. For a time I rested on it, read in my Milton and wrote in my notebook a reminder to commemorate this tree which had so charitably refreshed a tired wanderer. As you will see from this paragraph, I have now done it.

The little English miles are delightful to walk; you are so glad to be able to put a mile behind you so quickly; but as all miles are miles the smallness of the English mile is a deception. I reckon that if I walk at a normal pace I can cover six English miles in two hours and expend in the process almost the same effort as going one German mile – taking into consideration the specially good quality of the English roads. But it is a pleasant deception to see that one has gone twelve miles in only a few hours.

I estimate that I was about seventeen miles from London when I came to an inn where I had to pay sixpence for a little wine and water. An Englishman who sat near mine host recognized me for a German, and so from the same country as his queen, whom he extolled with a lavish spate of praise, saying that England had never before had such a queen and would not easily have another like her.

As it now began to grow hot, I found a clear brook on the left-hand side, not far from the highway, and after I had bathed in it I set out on my way again.

The heath was now behind me and there opened out before me the paradisal district towards Slough, lying twenty and a half miles on the road to Oxford from London. From there a road goes left to Windsor, whose high white castle I could already see in the distance.

I did not stop here but kept to the right, straight along a very pleasant road between meadows and green hedges towards Windsor [along a different road]. There I arrived at midday.

Passing through an English town is very strange to a foreigner because he fails to notice any of the things which distinguish a town from a village in a country like Germany. There are no fortifications – town walls, gate, or the like; no exciseman on the lookout, no menacing sentry to beware of; you pass through town and village as freely and unhindered as through wide-open Nature.

Just before Windsor lies Eton College, a famous public school, of which – as I have already stated – there are but few in England. It lay to my left, and immediately opposite was an inn.

I entered the inn.

This must have been at the boys' recreation time, for they were running about in the college courtyard – a great crowd. The courtyard was surrounded by a low wall.

They all wore the same remarkable dress, from the biggest to the smallest – a black mantle or gown through which the arms could be stuck – over their coloured clothing, and a square hat covered with velvet such as the clergy wear in some German towns.

They were doing all sorts of things: talking together, strolling about, and some had books in their hands and were reading. I soon had to get out of their sight, however, for they stared at me so, coming along as I did all covered with dust and with my staff in my hand.

As I entered the inn and asked for something to eat I could see at once from the expression of the waiter that I was unwelcome. They served me like a beggar, with muttering and neglect, but charged me like a gentleman. I honestly believe the fellow thought it not proper for him to wait on a miserable mortal who went afoot. I was tired and demanded a room to sleep in. They showed me one that looked like a lock-up for malefactors. I ordered a better room for the night and got the answer that they had no intention of putting me up for the night. It was not convenient. If I chose to go back to Slough I should easily find a night's lodging there.

It irritated me that I should be treated in this way when I had money in my pocket, even if I were a pedestrian. They made me pay two shillings for my lunch and coffee. I had already thrown it down and wanted nothing more than to shake the dust of this place off my feet and forget it, when I saw the green hill of Windsor smiling at me, so friendly, that it seemed to be inviting me to visit it first and forget the unfriendliness of mankind.

I strode then through the streets of Windsor, until a steep path at last led me to the summit of its hill, right to the very wall of the castle. There I saw a prospect so wide, so delightful and heart-uplifting that in a moment I had forgotten all my thoughts about the insults and injustice of men. Before me spread the realm of rich, abundant Nature, surely one of the most beautiful landscapes in the world! The stuff the muse of Pope had chosen lay at my feet, unrolled before my gaze majestically. What more could I have wished for in that moment?

And the venerable castle, bearing all the marks of grey antiquity, smiled through its green trees like an aged man whose hoary brow has been kept young by happiness.

Nothing inspired me with more reverence than St George's Chapel, which lies on the right as you come down from the castle; it raised within me by its very appearance memories of the centuries that had flowed past while it had stood.

But let me never more suffer the chagrin of being told about such marvels by insensitive timeservers who have learnt their speech by rote and troll it forth unwillingly a hundred times a day. The disgusting boor who showed me round the chapel for a shilling ruined the impression of the place itself by his claptrap. Henry VIII, Charles I and Edward IV lie buried here. Outside and inside, the chapel has an aspect of the deepest melancholy.

Building was going on at the royal palace and a great many workmen were busy with masses of stone which lay round about.

I went down a gentle slope to Windsor Park, wherein the dim light surrounds you like the atmosphere of a temple. This forest surpasses anything you can imagine of this sort, for to its natural charms were added the peace of solitude, the cool evening air and soft music coming down from the distant castle. All this was like a pleasant enchantment which compensated me a thousand times for all the setbacks of that day.

As I returned from the woods the clock struck six and the workmen were all going home.

I have forgotten to mention the great round tower of the ancient castle. The paths radiating out from this tower are lined with bushes, the green of which makes a pleasant contrast with the old stone of the building. Right on top of the tower the flag of Britain was being hauled down. As I left the castle I saw the King driving up in a plain coach. Apparently the people here are more polite than in London, for every man took off his hat as the King went by.

Arriving again in the town I found an imposing inn not far from the castle, where I saw some officers and other people of good standing going in and out. Contrary to my expectation I was received here without any fuss or bother by a landlord who himself seemed to be a man of importance. A very great difference from the surly way I had been greeted at the unsociable inn opposite Eton College.

Only – right from the first, it seemed my fate to be a

shock and eyesore to the servants. The maid muttered as she showed me to a room where I could tidy up my dress a little.

Afterwards I went back to the coffee-room, near the main entrance, and told the landlord that I should like to go for another short walk. He told me that right behind the inn was a pleasant field by way of which I could reach the bank of the Thames and a good bathing-place.

I followed his advice. So this evening proved as nice, if not nicer, than the foregoing one in Richmond. I found that the Thames wound softly here as elsewhere and that Windsor showed more beautifully from its green valley than did the houses on the hill at Richmond; the Windsor green was so soft and delicate. The field between the inn and the river sloped rather steeply. I sat behind a bush and awaited the setting of the sun. In the distance I saw many people bathing in the Thames.

After sundown, when some of the bathers had left, I drew near to the river and for the first time bathed in the Thames's cool flood. The bank here was rather steep, so they had built a flight of steps down into the water for the benefit of bathers who could not swim. A pair of red-cheeked young apprentices strolled down from the town, had their clothes off in a wink and dived in. They cut through the water with their sinewy arms until they were tired. Confidingly they advised me to untie my hair so that I too could dive in as they did.

Refreshed and stimulated by the cool bathe, I went for yet another walk in the moonlight along the river bank; on my left stood the towers of Windsor, in front of me a little village with its church spire sticking up above the trees; in the distance loomed two most attractive hills which I resolved to climb in the morning, and all around me were the cornfields. Oh, how indescribably beautiful was this evening and this walk! And there in the distance I could see my inn between the houses and I felt I had a refuge there, a place to return to, where I would be at home and could always stay.

But this sweet dream flew suddenly away as I came back to that home and saw the black looks of the waiters, who presumably expected not much in the way of a tip from me. My astonishment was greatest when the surly maid who had previously shown me to my room, met me in the parlour downstairs and told me with a mocking curtsey that I must find myself another lodging for the night; I could not stay there because she had shown me to a room already engaged.

Of course I protested (as you will guess), until at last the landlord came. I appealed to him. He at once let me have another room, but one which I should have to share with another guest. So here in Windsor I was almost turned out of doors a second time.

Right under this bedroom was a tap-room. The floor shook. Drinking songs were sung in which some passages occurred similar to some in our German *Trinklieder*. That much I could understand. The company consisted of officers such as I had seen before. I was hardly able to sleep with such a noise and bustle, and had just dozed off a little when my sleeping partner arrived, possibly one of those from the tap-room, and knocked into my bed as he searched for his own. With great difficulty he found it and threw himself on to it just as he was – clothes, boots and all.

This morning I got up very early in order to carry out my resolve to climb the two hills which had so attracted me yesterday. One especially intrigued me: it had on its summit a tall white house visible between the dark trees. The other hill lay right beside it.

I found no regular path leading to this hill, so I made straight towards its top, without taking notice of possible roads but keeping my direction. This was somewhat tiresome as I often had to go round a fence or round a marshy patch of earth, but finally I arrived at the foot of the hill with the high white house – the hill I wanted to climb. Then, as I was starting to climb it and was already congratulating myself on the view I should have from the white house, I read on a signboard: 'Take care! Steel traps and Spring-Guns are laid here!'

So my effort was all in vain. I went now to the other hill, but here again steel traps and spring-guns were laid for a wanderer whose only wish was to enjoy the beautiful morning on this high ground.

I went back to the town with my hopes as disappointed as my wish had been on Richmond Hill yesterday morning.

Arriving at the inn I received a sweet welcome from the ill-tempered maid, to the effect that under no circumstances could I lodge there another night. Anyway I had no such intention. At this moment I am writing to you from the coffee-room where a couple of Germans who imagine I don't know what they are saying, are talking. I have made myself known to them but the fellows don't consider me fit to talk to because I'm a walker! I think they're Hanoverians! – The weather is so fine that despite the little inconveniences I have been subjected to I shall continue my journey on foot.

TEN

On to Nettlebed:
the perfect village

Oxford, June 25th

BY WHAT A FATE is the wanderer beset in this land of horses and carriages! And what adventures!

Still, I only want to tell my tale properly from the beginning.

For an old hen I ate at supper, for a bedroom given to me grudgingly and in which I was pestered by a besotted oaf, and for two cups of tea at breakfast, I had to pay in Windsor nine shillings – and the old hen alone came to six shillings!

When I was about to leave, the waiter who had served me so unwillingly and with such ill temper stood at the foot of the stairs and said: 'Remember the waiter.'

I gave him three halfpence, to which he returned a hearty 'God damn you, sir!'

At the door stood the surly maid who said: 'Remember the chambermaid.'

'I'll remember your civility,' I said, and gave her nothing.

At this she vented her anger in a loud, coarse laugh. So I left Windsor followed by a flood of curses and derision.

How happy was I now to have the towers of Windsor behind me! It is not good for a wanderer to be near the palace of a king; so I sat down in the shadow of a hedge and read my Milton, whom I could trust to commend me to the true aristocracy of Nature.

I took my way again through Slough and continued by Salthill and Maidenhead. Right at the very end of Salthill village — if indeed it can be called that — a wigmaker had a booth in which he was shaving and hairdressing. I had to pay him a shilling to shave me and put my hair a bit more in order. His booth was opposite to a very elegant house and garden.

Between Salthill and Maidenhead the first of my adventures on this journey came my way.

As yet I had met hardly a single pedestrian, though coaches rolled past me continuously; for the Oxford road is very busy. I met also many people on horseback, which is here the usual mode of travel.

The road lay through a deep gulley between high trees, so I could not see far ahead, when a man in a brown coat, with a round hat and a stick in his hand a good deal stouter than mine, came towards me. From the first he struck me as suspicious, but he passed me by. But before I was aware of it he suddenly turned and demanded a halfpenny — only a halfpenny — to buy beer, because his belly was empty.

I felt in my pocket but found that I had no coppers, nor even a single sixpence, but I had plenty of shillings.

I excused myself for having no small change, whereupon he said: 'God bless my soul!' and clenched his fist on his stick so deliberately that I at once put my hand in my pocket again and gave him a shilling.

At that moment a coach came by.

He thanked me very politely and went away.

Had that coach arrived a moment sooner I should not so easily have given him a shilling I could ill spare. I do not want to assert that this man was a footpad, but he had every appearance of one.

I entered Maidenhead over the bridge of the same name, which is twenty-five miles from London. The English milestones are a great convenience for travellers; they have often seemed to relieve me of half the distance because I am always anxious to know how far I have come and if I am on the right road. The distance from London is always given on these milestones together with the distance to the next town, and at crossroads there is always a signpost, so it is almost impossible to lose your way. My journey was practically carefree.

From Maidenhead Bridge is a delightful view of a hill standing up from the bank of the Thames and crowned with two most splendid residences situated amid parks and meadows. The first is called Taplow and belongs to the Earl of Inchiquin. A little farther on lies Cliveden which also belongs to him. These mansions are set off charmingly by the surrounding fields and the thick woods.

It is not far from this bridge to Maidenhead, where there is another delightful country seat on the left as you enter the town, belonging to Pennyston Powney, Esq.

This information I have gained for the most part from my English Guide-book, which is almost continually in my hand and contains practically everything of note, mile by mile. I check the truth of the information with those with whom I stay, and they wonder how I, a foreigner, am so familiar with their district.

Maidenhead itself is a place of little note. I asked them to make me a mulled ale and had to pay ninepence for it. They evidently didn't take me for a man of much consequence, for I heard one say as I passed: 'A lusty comrade!', and the tone of it did not sound very creditable.

At the end of the village a shoemaker had his shop, just as had the barber at Salthill.

I went from here to Henley, eleven miles from Maidenhead and thirty-six from London.

When I had gone six English miles fairly quickly and was still five from Henley, I came to a piece of rising ground where stood a milestone. There I sat down to enjoy one of the most ravishing views. I certainly advise anyone who comes to this spot to make a point of seeing it. *

Close in front of me was a gentle hill, patterned with cornfields fenced with hedges and encircled above by a wood. Behind it in the distance there rose up from the opposite side of the Thames one green hill after another embellished with woodlands, meadows, hedges and villages. At their feet the river slid in delightful curves through a rich green valley studded with villages and elegant houses.

The banks of the Thames are fascinating everywhere, but especially so after a little separation, when you suddenly catch sight of it again with all its rich adjoining lands.

In the valley below the flocks were grazing and the sound of bells came up to me on the hill.

What makes such an English spot so magically beautiful is the blending of everything into a composition that ensures

* The view is still the same and can be seen from the clubhouse of Temple Golf Club.

a peaceful prospect. There is no spot on which the eye does not long lovingly to rest. After what I have already seen of the English countryside, what is merely average here would be regarded as a paradise in other lands.

With my heart inspired by this rewarding scene I went on up and down hill at a sharp pace for the remaining five miles to Henley. I arrived there at four in the afternoon.

Just short of Henley, on the left, standing on a hill rising up from the near bank of the river, is a country house within a park, the residence of General Conway. I walked a little way along the opposite bank of the Thames from where the park lay, before I went into Henley itself, and lay down in some tall grass. Being somewhat tired I went to sleep. When I awoke I found that the last rays of the setting sun were shining straight into my face.

Refreshed by this sweet slumber I went on again into the town. But my experience suggested it was too grand a place for me to stay in, and that I should do better to put up at a roadside inn of the kind the Vicar of Wakefield called 'the usual retreat of Indigence and Frugality'.

Only, the worst of it was that nobody wanted to take me into a refuge such as that. I met two farmers on the way; I asked the first of them if I should find hospitality for the night in a house which I saw in the distance by the wayside. 'I dare say you may,' was his reply. But when I came to it the answer was, 'We have got no beds, and you can't stay here tonight!'

It was the same at the next house I called at on the road. So I had to make up my mind to go on for another five miles to Nettlebed. There I arrived late in the evening; in fact it was already dark.

Everything was going swimmingly in this little village. Some soldiers on leave were making music after their own fashion. The very first house on the left on entering the village proved to be an inn with a crossbeam extending across the road to the house opposite and from which an astonishingly large signboard hung displaying the name of the proprietor.

'May I stay here the night?' was my first question as I came up to the house.

'Yes, you may,' was the answer. It was spoken coldly but under the circumstances it cheered me greatly.

They showed me into the kitchen and put me to eat at a table with soldiers and domestic servants. Thus I found myself for the first time in the sort of kitchen which figures so often in the novels of Fielding, and in which so many adventures usually take place.

The open fireplace where the cooking was done was separated from the rest of the kitchen by a wooden partition. Thus screened, the rest of the room served as a combined living and eating-room. All round its walls were shelves for pewter dishes and plates, while from the ceiling hung an abundance of provisions such as loaves of sugar, sausages, sides of bacon, and so on.

While I was eating, a post-chaise drove up to the inn, and immediately the whole household started into motion to receive the distinguished guests they heard approaching. But the gentlemen got out for only a moment, called for nothing more than a couple of pots of beer and then drove on again. But if you come in a post-chaise you are treated with all possible respect!

Although this was but a small village and they knew me to be a guest of no distinction, they nevertheless put me in a carpeted bedroom with a good bed.

The following morning I put on the clean linen I was carrying with me and came downstairs. This time they did not show me into the kitchen as on the previous evening, but into the parlour on the ground floor, and called me 'sir'. On the previous evening it had been 'master', by which term only the farmers and common people are addressed.

It was Sunday and everyone in the house had put on his best clothes. I found myself extraordinarily drawn to this pleasant village and resolved to stay and attend divine service that morning. To this end I borrowed a prayer-book from my host, Mr Illing. (This was his name! It struck me the more because it is such a common name in Germany.) I turned over the leaves during breakfast and read several parts of the English liturgy. My attention was taken by the fact that every word was set down for the priest for his conformity. If he were visiting a sick man, for example, he had to say 'Peace dwell in this house,'* etc.

That such a book is called a prayer-book and not a hymn-book is because the English service is usually not sung but prayed. Nevertheless the Psalms translated into English verse are included in this prayer-book.

That which my host lent me was truly a family possession containing the date of his wedding and the birthdays and baptismal days of all his children. It had all the more value consequently in my eyes.

Divine service was due to begin at half-past nine. Right opposite our house the boys of the village were lined up all bright and beautiful, very nice and clean, and their hair (cut round in a fringe after the English fashion) combed. The white collars of their shirts were turned back at both sides and their breasts were open to the air. It seemed they were gathered here at the entrance of the village to await the parson.

* 'Peace be to this house and to all that dwell in it' — *Book of Common Prayer*.

I went out of the village for a short walk towards where I saw some men coming from another village to attend divine service in ours.

At last the parson* arrived on horseback. The boys took off their hats and bowed low to him. He had a somewhat elderly appearance, with his own hair dressed very much as if in natural curls.

The bell rang and I went into the church with the general public, my prayer-book under my arm. The clerk or verger showed me into a seat in front of the pulpit very politely.

The furnishing of the church was quite simple. Right above the altar were displayed the Ten Commandments in large letters on two tablets. And indeed there can be no better way of impressing the essential qualities of the faith on a waiting congregation than this.

Under the pulpit was a reading-desk where the preacher stood before the sermon and read out a very long liturgy to which the parish clerk responded each time, the congregation joining in softly. When, for example, the preacher said: 'God have mercy upon us,' the clerk and congregation answered: 'and forgive us our sins'. Or the preacher read a prayer and the whole congregation said 'Amen' to it.

This is very difficult for the preacher, since he must not only address the people while preaching his sermon but continually do so during the service. The responding of the people, however, has something about it very restful and ceremonially appropriate.

Two soldiers sitting by me, who had recently come from London and considered themselves to be keen wits, did not pray aloud.

After the ritual had gone on for some time I noticed

* The Reverend John Reade.

some shuffling in the choir.* The clerk was very busy and they all seemed to be getting ready for some special ceremony. I noticed also several musical instruments of various sorts as the preacher stopped his reading and the clerk announced from the choir: 'Let us praise God by singing the forty-seventh Psalm. "Awake, our hearts, awake with joy".'†

How peaceful and heart-uplifting it was to hear vocal and instrumental music in this little country church, not made by hired musicians but joyfully offered by the happy dwellers in the place in praise of their God. This kind of music now began to alternate several times with the ritual prayers, and the tunes of the metrical psalms were so lively and joyful – and yet so wholly sincere – that I gave my heart unrestrainedly to devotion and was often touched to tears.

The preacher now stood up and gave a short address on the text: 'Not all who say "Lord! Lord!" shall enter into the Kingdom of Heaven.' He dealt with the subject in common terms and his presentation was sturdy. He spoke of the need to do God's will, but there was nothing out of the usual run in his matter. The sermon lasted less than half-an-hour.

Apart from all this the preacher was unsociable; he seemed haughty when he acknowledged the greetings of the country people, doing so with a superior nod.

I stayed until the service was all over and then went out of the church with the congregation. I then examined the gravestones in the churchyard and their inscriptions, which, because of their restraint, were simpler and in better taste than ours.

Some, to be sure, were frank enough – even comical.

* In the west gallery.

† Moritz is mistaken: this was their anthem, not Psalm 47.

One on the gravestone of a blacksmith* I have set down in writing so that you can't prove it is not so:

> My Sledge and Anvil lie declined,
> My bellows too have lost their Wind;
> My Fire's extinct, my Forge decayed,
> And in the Dust my Vice is laid;†
> My Coals are spent, my Iron's gone,
> My Nails are drove: my Work is done.

Many inscriptions I found ending with the following rhyme:

> Physicians were in vain;
> God knew the best
> And laid his Dust to rest.

In the church itself I saw the marble epitaph to a son of the famous Dr Wallis‡ with the following simple, peaceful inscription:

That Learning and Good Sense which rendered HIM
fit for any Publick Station Induc'd Him to choose a
Private Life.

All the farmers I saw here were dressed in good cloth and good taste. (Not as ours are, in coarse smocks.) In appearance they are to be distinguished from townsmen less by their dress than by their natural dignity.

A few soldiers trying to show off joined me as I was looking at the church. They seemed thoroughly ashamed – saying it was a most contemptible church. At this I took the

---

* William Strange.
† This line Moritz omitted.
‡ Dr John Wallis, Savilian Professor of Geometry in Oxford (1649–1703).

liberty to tell them that no church was contemptible if it held well-behaved and sensible people.

I remained in Nettlebed over midday. In the afternoon there was no divine service but the villagers again made music together. They sang several psalms while others listened to them. All this was done in so seemly a manner that it might have been a kind of service too. I stayed until it was over, as one enchanted by this village. Three times I started to leave it to continue my walk, and each time I was drawn back to it, on the verge of resolving to stay there a week or longer.

Yet the thought that I had only a few weeks to spare before my return to Germany, and that I still wanted to see Derbyshire, drove me finally forth. I looked back often at the little church tower and the tranquil cottages where I had been so much at home; and I looked back with a heavy heart.

It was nearly three o'clock in the afternoon as I went away from Nettlebed. Oxford was eighteen miles away, so I decided not to go right there but to stay the night some five or six miles short of Oxford and reach the city in good time on the following morning.

My journey from Nettlebed was as an uninterrupted stroll through a great garden. Often I turned from the road and read some Milton. When I was come without mishap about eight miles from Nettlebed and was not far from Dorchester, and had the Thames on my left, I saw at some distance beyond it a long hill with what appeared to be the mast of a ship standing up from behind it. This led me to suppose that another river ran on the other side of the hill.

This promised me a view which I would not willingly pass by the way. I turned off the road to the left, crossed a bridge over the Thames and then went up the hill towards the mast. When I got to the top, however, I found that the whole thing was an optical illusion. Before me lay nothing but a great plain and the mast was stuck in the ground to entice the curious from the road.

So I descended the hill again. At its foot was a house with many people looking out of the window and apparently laughing at me, but this affected me very little and I went on my way. The journey to the mast had not grieved me but I was rather tired from the climb. *

Not far from there – near to Dorchester – I had yet another richly rewarding scene. The country became so beautiful that I had no wish to go farther, but lay down on the green turf and feasted my eyes on the view as if enchanted. The moon had already risen and stood at the full; the sun's last rays were darting through the hedges; and as if these were not enough there came a sleepy fragrance from the meadows and the song of the birds. The hills by the Thames revealed their many shades of green – bright green, pale green, dark green – with the tufted tops of trees here and there among them. I nearly fainted under the spell of all these ravishing delights.

Dorchester, where I arrived rather late, is only a small village but it has a large and imposing church. As I went by, this place also seemed too grand for me; the ladies stood in front of their houses with their hair trimmed.

* The hill must have been Sinodun (or Wittenham Clumps), but why did not Moritz remark on the magnificent ancient earthworks on the summit?

ELEVEN
The friendly dons

Oxford, June 25th (*continued*)

SO I DECIDED to go on for another four and a half miles to Nuneham – itself only five miles from Oxford. There I arrived in the gloomy night and rather tired.

The place consists of two rows of close-built houses laid as regularly in line as a London street. All their doors were shut and only a few houses showed a light.

But right at the end of the village I caught sight of a huge sign hanging out over the road. The last house on the left was an inn, and there everyone was still astir.

I entered without ceremony and said that I wanted to stay for the night.

'By no means,' they said. The idea was impossible; the whole house was full; all their beds were engaged; since I had come so far I might as well go on five miles to Oxford.

Being so hungry I demanded that at least they should give me something to eat, but I only got the answer that since I shouldn't be staying there the night it wouldn't be fair for them to feed me. I could go farther on and sup where I slept.

Then I demanded a pot of beer, which they deigned to give me for ready money, but a bite of bread – for which I also would gladly have paid cash – they refused me.

Such astonishing inhospitality I hadn't expected even at an English inn. But I now wanted to try everything possible in order to discover how far the uncharitable nature of these people would go. I begged them to let me sleep on a bench, for which I would pay as much as for a bed, for I was so tired that I couldn't go on any longer.

Even as I made this plea they slammed the door in my face.

Since they wouldn't put me up in a small village, what better treatment could I expect in Oxford? I made up my mind to spend the night in the open, for it was quite warm. I had actually found myself a comfortable spot under a tree and was taking off my overcoat to lay under my head as a pillow, when I heard someone coming up behind me with rapid steps and shouting to me: 'If you will wait, we can go along together.'

Little as anyone is to be trusted who follows you into a field in the gloomy night, yet in my predicament anyone was a friend who concerned himself with another human being and wanted to walk along with me in a place so extraordinarily unfriendly to all mankind. I waited quietly for him, and as he came up to me he said that he also was going to Oxford, and if I was a good walker we could go along together. I assured him that I was and we accordingly set off together.

Now I did not know if my fellow-traveller was to be trusted, so I took the first opportunity to inform him that I was a poor wanderer, so much so that I had suffered the injustice of being refused shelter in the last inn I had called at and had even been refused a bite of bread although I had offered to pay for it.

He excused the people there, saying that truly the house was full of men working in the area, but he added that he himself couldn't approve of anybody being refused a piece of bread. He asked me how far I had come that day.

I answered, 'From Nettlebed', and told him that I had attended divine service there that morning.

'Since you probably came through Dorchester this afternoon,' he said, 'you might have heard me preach, too, if you had gone into the church; for Dorchester is my vicarage, from which I have just come, and I'm on my way back to Oxford.'

'So you are a clergyman?' said I, full of joy to have fallen in with a traveller of my own sort on such a dark night. I gave him to understand that I was not travelling on foot for reasons of poverty as I had earlier said, but in order to get to know the customs of the people.

He was as pleased with this agreeable meeting as I was, and we shook hands in eternal brotherhood before we went any farther.

Then he started to say a few words in Latin, and when I answered him in Latin spoken after the manner of the English he gave me his approval of my pronunciation. He said that once, several years ago, he had met another German, also in the dead of night and almost in the same spot, and they had spoken to each other in Latin, but the German had pronounced it so badly that he had only understood a few words of it.

Our conversation now turned to theology and, among other things, the new teachings of Dr Priestley, whom he condemned to the lowest pit of hell. I was on my guard and agreed with him on this text; I greatly won his favour by approving his contentions without reserve.

During the course of this conversation we walked nearly to Oxford without noticing the tediousness of the way.

'Now,' said he, 'you will soon see one of the most beautiful and superb cities not merely in England but in all Europe. Only it's a pity you'll miss the nobility of the scene because it's dark.'

This I certainly did miss, for I saw nothing of the glory of Oxford until after we had settled in. Then he said, as we entered the city, that I should see one of the longest, most superb and beautiful streets not only in this city nor in England, but in the whole of Europe.

To see the beauty and the splendour of that street was not vouchsafed me, but of its length I took full note as we went ever along it. Unless the longest street in Europe came to an end, or I found out where in this famous street I could stay the night –

But at last my companion stood still and said he now wanted to leave me and go to his college, where he lived.

I replied: 'And I will sit down on a stone and wait until the morning, for I shall only find an inn here with the greatest difficulty.'

'You want to sit on a stone!' he said, shaking his head. 'Better come with me to a tavern in the neighbourhood; possibly we shall run into some more company there.'

So we went on past a few more houses and knocked on a door. It had already gone twelve o'clock. Someone opened it, and what was my surprise on passing through a door in a wooden partition on the left, to see a whole roomful of clergymen in their gowns and cravats sitting round a great table with their beer-mugs in front of them, to whom my companion introduced me as a German clergyman and said he couldn't commend too highly my Latin pronunciation, my orthodoxy and my ability as a pedestrian.

This was a situation which could only come in a dream. I saw it at once. There was I, arrived in Oxford in the middle of the night and without knowing how, set down among a company of Oxford clergy.

While it happened I knew I ought to take advantage of the situation. I spoke about our German universities, and of how there was often unrest in them – noisy disturbances and the like.

'Oh, we have noisy disturbances here too, sometimes,' one of the clergymen assured me, banging the table with his hand.

The conversation grew ever more lively. One man asked me about Herr Bruns, the present professor at Helmstadt, who was known to most of the company.

Among these was a lay clerk who fancied himself as a wit and raised various quibbles against the Bible. His name was Clark and he made much play on it. ' "Clerk" also means "verger"; so I stick to being a "Clark" and never become a clergyman,' he said. On the whole he was of his kind – a droll fellow.

Among other things this Clark tried to catch my fellow-traveller – whom I heard addressed as 'Mr Modd' – by claiming that it was written quite plainly in the Bible that God was a wine-bibber.

At this Mr Modd lost his temper and declared that it would be absolutely impossible to find such a passage in the Bible. Another clergyman, named Caern, roped in his absent brother, forty years in the Church. He must know something of it if it were in the Bible, but he would swear his brother knew nothing of it.

'Waiter, fetch a Bible!' shouted Mr Clark. And a great

family Bible was brought and slammed down on the table amidst the ale mugs.

Mr Clark turned over a few pages and read in the Book of Judges ix, 13: 'Should I leave my wine, which cheereth God and man?' *

Mr Modd and Mr Caern, confident up to this time, now sat as if stupefied. For a few moments there was silence. Then the spirit of the Gregorians came over me and I said: 'Gentlemen, this is an allegorical expression.' Then I held forth on the theme of how often earthly kings were called gods in the Bible.

'Certainly it is an allegorical expression,' shot in at once Mr Modd and Mr Caern, 'and it is plain to see how such a thing is feasible.' Having thus triumphed over poor Clark they drank my health in long draughts.

But Mr Clark had not yet shot his last bolt and felt compelled to draw their attention to a passage in the Book of the Prophet Ezekiel which stated in plain words that God was a barber.

At this Mr Modd became so enraged that he called the clerk 'An impudent fellow!', and Mr Caern referred again to his absent brother – forty years in the Church – who would certainly have held Mr Clark to be a shameless cad to maintain any such abomination.

But Mr Clark remained calm and pointed out a passage in Ezekiel where anyone could read that it was said of the obdurate Jews: 'God will shave the beard of them.' †

* The full passage reads: 'And the vine said: "Should I leave my wine, which cheereth God and man, and go to be promoted over the trees?" '

† The English translator of Moritz (1795) has altered 'Ezekiel' to 'Isaiah chapter vii, v. 20'. Here they are: Ezekiel v, verse 1: 'And thou, son of man, take thee a sharp knife, take thee a

If at the clerk's previous quotation Mr Modd and Mr Caern beat their heads, they did so even more now. Even Mr Caern's brother – forty years in the Church – was deflated at this.

I broke the silence by saying: 'Gentlemen, that is another allegorical expression.'

'Certainly it is,' put in Mr Modd and Mr Caern in one voice, banging the table at the same time.

'If the prisoners,' I urged, 'were to have their beards cut, and since God had delivered them into the hands of foreigners, these their captors would cut off their beards.'

'That is understandable,' said one; 'it is as clear as the day.' And Mr Caern expressed his opinion that his brother – forty years in the Church – would explain it even so.

After this second triumph over Mr Clark he remained quiet and made no further objection to the Bible. As for the rest of the company, some of them drank my health again in strong ale – highly obnoxious to me because it intoxicates nearly as much as wine.

The discussion moved on to other subjects until it was almost daylight and Mr Modd started up with a 'Damme! I must read prayers in All Souls College!'

---

barber's razor, and cause it to pass upon thine head, and upon thy feet.'

Isaiah viii, verse 20: 'In the same day shall the Lord shave with a razor that is hired, *namely*, by them beyond the river, by the King of Assyria, the head, and the hair of the feet: and it shall also consume the beard.' Moritz's remarks might apply to Isaiah, but he wrote 'Ezekiel'. But then he was tired and, shall we say, bemused.

TWELVE
Across the Midlands

Oxford, June 25th (continued)

BEFORE MR MODD LEFT he invited me to visit him the following morning and most politely offered to show me the features of interest in Oxford. The rest of the company broke up, too, and, since I had been one of such a respectable company – although, no doubt, a peculiar one – the landlord made no bones about taking me in and showed me to a good bedroom.

But when I awoke I had such a headache as a result of my heavy drinking to the reverend gentlemen that I could not possibly get up, much less visit Mr Modd in his college.

The inn I occupied was called the Mitre and I found there the most admirable service – quite contrary to Windsor. Only I must confess that before I went to bed, being in somewhat high spirits, I said straight out to the waiter that he need not think that because I was travelling on foot I should be miserly with my tip. I assured him to the contrary and received the best service in the world.

I now determined to stay in Oxford for two days and

while there to order clean linen. This is especially important here. In the afternoon, as I was out walking in linen not too clean, I heard two women talking at their doors in a small street: 'Look at that fine gentleman,' said one, 'and he prefers to wear not even a clean shirt!'

I ate downstairs with the family and a few others who had dropped in for a meal and the conversation pleased me greatly. I had to tell them a great deal about Germany and especially about the King of Prussia. My decision to tramp the country they approved, but it set them wondering a great deal, and in the end they told me quite frankly that they would not have put me up had I not arrived there under special circumstances. Anyone else who travelled so far afoot would be regarded as a beggar or a rogue. From that I could easily explain my reception at Windsor and Nuneham, though I disapprove greatly of this terribly exaggerated respect for luxury which marks out any pedestrian in England for a disreputable man.

As I wanted to go on to Derbyshire now, I was advised to book a seat in a stage-coach – at least until I got farther into the country. The farther from London the less the standard of comfort and refinement; the more economical it would therefore be. So I resolved to travel by coach from Oxford to Birmingham, where I had an introduction from Mr Pointer of London to a merchant named Fothergill. After that I would proceed on foot.

I spent Monday rather unsatisfactorily because of my headache. Mr Modd came personally to take me away because he wanted to keep his promise, only I found myself in no condition to go with him.

Nevertheless towards evening I went another short walk, up a hill that lies to the north of Oxford and from which the whole city can be seen. It didn't seem to me however to be by far so magnificent as Mr Modd had described it on our nocturnal walk.

The colleges are built of grey stone, mostly in the Gothic style and much overlaid with ornament. The stone may have looked better when new, but now it has the most disgustingly repugnant colour one can imagine.

Only a few of these colleges are modern in construction and the other houses are contemptible in the extreme, with shingle roofs. Oxford bears a melancholy aspect and I cannot understand how anyone can regard it as one of the finest cities in England next to London.

I waited on the hill until the sun went down. Near me was a flight of steps which went down to a subterranean passage. I saw various students going for walks, with large black gowns over their coloured clothing, and square flat hats just like the scholars at Eton. This is the costume of all who belong to the university. There are slight differences in it to distinguish their academic degrees and social ranks. The wearing of a gown distinguishes also between members of the university – 'gownsmen' – and men of the city – 'townsmen'. If you want to include everyone in Oxford you say 'the whole city – gownsmen and townsmen'.

Certainly this dress is more seemly than the big top-boots, cockades in the hat, waistcoats and hunting-whips affected by some of our students. Equally surprising is the general calmness and modest behaviour of Oxford students.

As promised, Mr Modd showed me next day some of the interesting features of Oxford. He took me first to his rooms in college, which seemed very like a cell, being on the ground floor and very low and gloomy. These were in Corpus Christi College.

Afterwards he took me to All Souls College, an elegant building with a particularly beautiful chapel. Mr Modd pointed out to me a picture by Mengs, over the altar, * at the sight of which he showed more artistic perception than I had given him credit for. He said that every time he looked on that picture he was touched.

The picture shows Mary Magdalene at the moment when she suddenly sees Jesus standing before her, and falls down before him. On her face are all the human passions – pain, joy, grief – depicted so masterfully that one can never tire of gazing on it – and the more you gaze the more you will be emotionally moved.

He showed me also the library of this college, provided with a gallery, and all of it most beautifully designed. Among the books I saw here was an illustrated description of Oxford; the copper-plate prints certainly showed the towers and general architecture of Oxford to be finer on paper than in reality.

From All Souls Mr Modd took me to the Bodleian Library, which may be compared with the Vatican at Rome, and then to the building called the Theatre where official disputations are held. This is a round building fitted with rows of benches around its walls, each row raised higher than that in front of it; on these the doctors, masters and undergraduates sit, and in the midst two rostrums are built right opposite to each other, from which the disputants address each other.

Christ Church College and Queen's College are the most modern and beautiful of the public buildings. Beliol's (*sic*) College seems to be commendable for its antiquity and completely Gothic style.

Mr Modd told me that there are a lot of odd jobs to be had preaching in Oxford. Every undergraduate of a certain

* 'Noli me tangere', by Raphael Mengs of Madrid. The picture is now by the south door of the antechapel.

academic standing must preach one sermon on a Sunday in the University Church, but most of them find a substitute when their turn comes round and pay him as much as five to six guineas for a sermon.

He also told me that he had been in the university for eighteen years and could become a doctor as soon as he chose. He was a Master of Arts and lecturer on classical literature, besides being an ordained clergyman taking divine services in several villages round Oxford.

On our way we met the poet Warton,* now an elderly man but still Fellow of a college. Mr Modd told me that after poetry his greatest delight is in shooting wild duck.

Taken on the whole Mr Modd appears to be a good humanitarian. He told me that the Parish Clerk in Dorchester had died leaving a large family in dire need. He was going to ride out there the following day to get the late clerk's son – a lad of sixteen – appointed to the clerkship, in order to relieve the family distress.

Dons and undergraduates are always dropping into the Mitre for a chat, a pot of ale and a short parley with the landlord's daughter. She is a well-behaved wench.

They praised greatly a German named Mitchel (at least that is how they pronounced his name) who has been famous for many years as a musician. I was surprised and much pleased to hear of a fellow-countryman so renowned among the English, and went to see him, but he was not at home.

Castleton, June 30th

Before I tell you anything about the place where I am now, I want to set out the story of my adventures on the way. So I shall start where I left off in my last letter.

* Tom Warton: historian of poetry. Became Poet Laureate in 1785. Fond of low company – bargees, etc.

On Tuesday afternoon Mr Modd took me along the walks in Oxford and remarked fairly often that none more beautiful could be found not merely in England but in the whole of Europe. Certainly there were some remarkably pretty paths, especially a short walk behind Corpus Christi College along by the river.

We sat on a seat in this avenue and Mr Modd drew from his pocket a newspaper in which among other things was a review of a German book by Prof. Beckmann of Göttingen. The book was praised in the review and Mr Modd showed some respect for German literature. Then we parted; he to get the post of parish clerk of Dorchester filled and I to the Mitre to get ready for my departure from Oxford. I left on the early morning coach at three o'clock after paying a moderately cheap bill, very reasonable for what I had received.

When the coach started there was with me inside only a young man dressed in black; the cockade in his hat proclaimed him an officer. The outside of the coach was occupied by women and soldiers. The common women hereabouts wear short cloaks of red cloth, but hats like those of their betters.

All English women, from the humblest servant girl, follow the fashion in hats, which is in my opinion far better than that in hoods and caps worn by our German middle-class women. The distinction in dress among the various classes is not really so great.

I had something of a headache and consequently may have seemed to my travelling companion like a hater of mankind. Or he may have thought me reserved (which was possibly more or less natural to him, an Englishman).

He spoke to me once in a very friendly manner, but I showed not the slightest interest in starting a conversation.

From his behaviour I gathered that he was sympathetic towards one in my condition.

He told me that he had studied medicine but was now on the point of travelling to the East Indies to try his luck as an officer. He was first going to Birmingham to take leave of his three sisters who lived there in a boarding-school.

To gain his confidence I told him of my adventures in tramping through England. He thought this method surprisingly courageous but approved it when he knew my reason for doing it. I asked him why the English didn't occasionally go on foot themselves and he answered: 'They are too rich and too lazy.'

And it is true that the poorest of them would rather sit on the outside of a coach at the risk of breaking his neck than go for a stretch on foot. It frightened me when the coach stopped and one of the women riding outside began to get down; for just as she was doing so the horses unexpectedly started off again and she was in danger of a terrible fall.

From Oxford to Birmingham is sixty-two miles, but they were all lost to me because I was in a coach again — whisked at breakneck speed from one village to another; the very antithesis of what I regard as travel.

My travelling companion made some amends for this loss. He seemed to be a good-humoured man and I felt easily drawn to him. And so it was with him; we behaved as if our friendship was firmly established.

We quite fortuitously got into a discussion about Shakespeare and then, all at once, found ourselves in Stratford-upon-Avon, Shakespeare's birthplace, where the coach stopped to change horses. We were still twenty-two miles from Birmingham and ninety-four from London.

Here our sentiments took on new life. In this place was

born possibly the greatest genius that Nature has produced; in this place he fed his young mind; on these fields he played as a boy, and when he had retired from the greater theatre of the world whose manners, hopes and vices he had so masterfully portrayed, it was to this place he returned to spend the last years of his life contentedly with his chosen friends; among these humble cottages.

The Avon is fairly broad, and along its bank stretches a row of cottages only a single storey high and roofed with shingles. Simplicity and contentment is the theme they seem to suggest.

We saw Shakespeare's house. It is one of the poorest, worst preserved and most unseemly houses in Stratford. And yet, under this mean roof he spent the happiest days of his life. In this house now live an old couple who make a living by showing it to strangers.

Shakespeare's chair, on which he used to sit in front of his door, is already so hacked away that barely anything of a chair is to be seen. For everyone who passes through this town cuts himself a chip off it to carry away as a relic. I cut off my bit, but it was too small and I have lost it. So you won't get it on my return.

I examined each spot closely as we went farther through the streets, for this is the country wherein a soul like Shakespeare's had been first awakened by the spirit of Nature. For the first impressions of childhood are always significant, forming as they do the basis of the thought which follows. And although the district is not especially beautiful it has on the whole something of a befitting romanticism.

We arrived in Birmingham at three in the afternoon, I having paid sixteen shillings at Stratford for my seat in the coach from Oxford to Birmingham. They had demanded nothing from me at Oxford. It is not the same in England as in Germany where posting charges have to be paid in advance.

My travelling companion and I got out at the inn where the coach stopped. We were sorry to part and I had to promise him that I would visit him on my return to London, for which purpose he gave me his address. His father is an author famous in his line, by name Dr Milson.

I inquired for the house of Mr Fothergill, to whom I had a letter of introduction, but only to learn that he had died eight days previously. Under these circumstances the introduction couldn't serve me very well and there was no purpose in my remaining in Birmingham.

Without more ado then I asked the way to Derby and got out of Birmingham almost as soon as I had reached it, so I can tell you nothing of this famous city of factories and organized industry.

The road out of Birmingham is not of the best, being rather sandy. I got as far as the small town of Sutton by that evening. It seemed too superior a place to spend the night until, right at the far end, I came to a small inn with the sign of the Swan and underneath the landlord's name and occupation – Aulton, Brickmaker.

This inn looked more inviting for such as I, so I went inside. I didn't immediately ask for accommodation, however, but ordered a pot of beer, or, as they say in those parts, 'a point of ale'. They addressed me as 'master' and sent me into the kitchen where the landlady sat at a table complaining of toothache. My sympathy for her misfortune soon put me in her good books, however, especially as I was a foreigner, and she herself asked me if I should like to stay there for the night. Of course I agreed. So again I had a shelter for the night.

There I met a woman chimney-sweeper and her children,

who at once drank my health very amiably and talked freely with me and the hostess.

This chimney-sweep told me her life-story, and very interesting it was. Early in her married life her husband had been pressed into the army and she had lost him. She assumed him dead and had then earned a living as a servant in Ireland without anyone knowing she was married. During this time her chimney-sweep husband had returned to England and set up in business in Lichfield. As soon as he was firmly established there he inquired on all hands for his wife and at last found out where she was. He not only fetched her home to her rightful place, but organized a splendid feast in her honour, for all the neighbours to welcome her. She lived with her husband in Lichfield, only a few miles from Sutton, respected by all and helping him with his work. She told me that Lichfield would be on my way the following morning.

During her absence the landlady told me in confidence that despite his wife's mean appearance the chimney-sweep could put his hand on a thousand pounds without reckoning his silver, pewter and copper plate; that he wore a silver watch, and when he passed through Sutton he always stayed there the night and paid like a nobleman.

By using the word 'nobleman' instead of 'gentleman' she meant that he behaved more like a peer.

The landlady also remarked that the chimney-sweep's wife was somewhat 'low-lived' but that he was, on the contrary, the best-behaved man in the world. Now I had faintly noticed that the speech of the woman chimney-sweep was somewhat coarse. For example, she pronounced the word 'old' as we should spell it in German '*auld*'. At this distance from London I had not as yet noticed any other divergence in appearance or speech.

The woman chimney-sweep said that she would not be

at home the next day, nor her husband, but she gave me their name and address and said that if I returned by way of Lichfield she would like me to honour them with a visit.

In the evening the rest of the landlady's family arrived – a son and a daughter – who did everything they could to ease their mother's suffering. I was treated just like one of the family – as naturally as if I had been living with them for years.

Happening to mention that I was a scholar, the son told me that there was a grammar-school in Sutton where the headmaster's salary was worth two hundred pounds a year apart from scholars' fees. And this was only a small place! I thought *en passant* of our 'grammar-schools' in Berlin and the pay of our 'schoolmasters'.

When I paid my bill the following morning I couldn't help but notice the great difference in their charges compared with Windsor, Nettlebed and Oxford. In Oxford I had to pay at least three shillings for supper, bed and breakfast, besides giving a shilling to the waiter. At Sutton I was charged only one shilling for supper, bed and breakfast, and when I gave the daughter of the house fourpence for doing the duties of a chambermaid she thanked me most politely and gave me in addition a written recommendation to an innkeeper in Lichfield with whom I could get good lodging – for in general the people of Lichfield are haughty. This letter of recommendation was a masterpiece of 'the new spelling', wherein you spell words exactly as they sound to you. It looks particularly odd in English!

I took my leave of this house promising as an old friend to visit them again on my return journey.

At midday I arrived in Lichfield – an old-fashioned town with dirty narrow alleys where for the first time I noticed they had round window-panes – unusual in England. The town bore, I thought, an unfriendly air. I therefore made no use of my recommendation but went straight through, pausing only at a bakery to buy some bread which I took with me on my way.

In the evening I reached Burton, where the famous ale is brewed. Before I got to this town I was already tired and intended therefore to stay for the night. But I soon gave up that idea. As soon as I got into the town I felt again that threat of exclusion, as when I was near to London. And yet the Burton people had such a small-town mentality, pointing their fingers at me – a walking stranger. I passed down a long street where all the people were standing at their doors on both sides, and I had to run the gauntlet of their curious gaze and hear behind me the sound of their hissing.

All my reassuring theories – that I should never see these people again, nor they me, and so on – did not help me at all. This state of affairs was well-nigh unbearable. The street seemed to be a mile long, and certainly tired me as much as if it were. Nowhere have I found such hated concentration on a passer-by as here in Burton. How happy was I to find myself once more out of it and in the open country, though I did not yet know where I should find shelter for the night. I was moreover extremely tired.

I went along the Derby road whither a footpath from Burton led me by way of a pleasant meadow with stiles to climb.

I went for a long way without coming to a wayside inn and it was now getting dark, so I sat down beside a small toll-house, resting on the lowest of a flight of steps put there to enable pedestrians to pass over the barrier of the toll-gate. I thought if need be the turnpike-man might offer me shelter.

After I had been sitting there some time a farmer rode

up and asked me where I wanted to go. I told him I was so tired I could go no farther, and in a moment this good man offered without suspicion to set me behind him on the horse and take me to the next inn where I could stay the night.

It was a tall cart-horse. And as I couldn't mount him at once, the turnpike-man came out – a man as old as the hills, by the look of him, whom I shouldn't have thought had enough strength to support himself – and yet this man took me by the arm and swung me up on to the horse!

So I trotted along with my excellent farmer, who didn't ask a single inquisitive question, but set me down before the inn and trotted off to his village somewhere on the left.

The inn was named the Bear. The landlord went about the company growling like a bear too. This bespoke a good reception only if I could soften him up a bit; so I ordered a pot of ale and drank twice with him. By this means I soon had him polite and talkative and was able to speak with him right pleasantly. This trick I had noted from *The Vicar of Wakefield*, who always made mine host convivial by inviting him to drink. Besides that it was better for me, because I can't stand strong ale.

He now called me 'sir' and made one of the servants lay a separate table for himself and me, saying that he saw plainly that I was a 'gentleman'.

We spoke a good deal of George II, his favourite king (George III had little of his credit), coming finally to the battle of Dettingen, of which he knew many of the details. And I had to tell him about the King of Prussia and his many soldiers, and the price of sheep in Prussia. After we had been talking some time he suddenly asked me if I could blow the hunting horn. This he expected me to be able to do because I came from Germany! He recollected that when he was a boy his parents had put up a German at this same inn, and this German had been able to blow the hunting horn very well. So he thought blowing the hunting horn to be an accomplishment of all Germans.

I put him right about this and we got back to the subject of politics, his children and servants listening respectfully from a polite distance.

So here again I spent a pleasant evening and in the morning, after I had breakfasted, I found my bill was no higher than at Sutton.

On Friday morning I reached the heath before Derby. The air was mild and I was cheerful and contented. Then towards midday I had my first view of the romantic scenery of that part of Derbyshire into which I proposed to go. I came to a great height from which I saw all at once the whole prospect of these hills before me. Hills near by were succeeded by hills behind them and these in turn were succeeded by others peering through the spaces in between.

Soon I was passing over these – up and down as if on a series of waves. At one moment I was taking in the joy of a wide prospect and at the next I was dipping into a deep hollow.

At midday I saw Derby in the valley in front of me. I was now a hundred and twenty-six miles from London. Derby is a small, unimposing town; it was market day and I had to make my way through a crowd of people, but here I suffered no such rude inquisitive stares as at Burton. From this time on, moreover, I was always greeted politely by the children whenever I passed through a village.

From Derby to Matlock Bath, in the midst of the romantic scenery, it was yet fifteen miles. On the way I passed through a long wide village which I believe is called Duffield, where I ate a cold lunch. They didn't put me in the kitchen but in a room.

Usually you find that the pictures and copperplate prints hung in English inns are portraits of the Royal Family in a group assembled round their father the King, or a map of London. The portrait of the King of Prussia I have found to be very popular in this district. Scenes by Hogarth are often also to be found. It was very hot and on that account I had often to listen to the pitying phrase 'God almighty' as I, a poor wanderer, came into their view.

In the evening I stayed at another roadside inn only four miles from Matlock. I could easily have gone on to Matlock that evening, but I wanted to save my first sight of that area for the morning light, rather than approach it in the dusk.

I was not so lucky in this inn, however, as I had been in the two previous ones. I should have drunk the health of the landlord immediately, but the kitchen was full of farmers and I couldn't tell who was the landlord. A woman who was in the kitchen said, 'Your health, gentlemen all', every time she drank, and I forgot to drink her health – I don't know why. This was taken as a slight. The landlord twice drank my health in a contemptuous manner, as if to rebuke my bad manners, and then started to comment on me to the rest of the company, who almost got to pointing at me with their fingers. So I had to serve as a butt for the sneers of the yokels until at last one of them said: 'We must do him no harm, for he is a stranger.' To excuse himself the landlord said 'It is no harm.' But he seemed to tone down a bit, bottling up his mockery. When I wished to drink his health he shrugged it off and said sneeringly to me that all I had to do was to sit by the fire and keep myself warm and not concern myself with the world. The landlady took pity on me and led me out of the kitchen into another room where I could be alone, saying at the same time: 'They're Godless folk!'

I left this unfriendly house early next morning and went to Matlock.

I had now definitely decided that my goal was to be the great cave at Castleton, in the High Peak of Derbyshire. This was only twenty miles from Matlock.

The earth looked very different here from what I had seen at Windsor and Richmond. Instead of green fields and gentle hills I now saw bare mountains and crags set off against the sky. Instead of green hedges round the fields, they were here enclosed with grey stone walls, and the houses, too, were of this same material, all locally quarried, in a similar traditional style of rough-hewn stones laid almost undressed one upon another in the shape of four walls. One could build such a house with little exertion. The houses in Derby are apparently built of this same stone.

The situation at Matlock itself surpassed all I had expected of it. On the right were several elegant houses for those taking treatment for their ailments at the baths. Smaller cottages hung on the rocks like nests. On the left ran the river in a deep ravine, almost hidden from sight under a high majestic arch of overhanging trees. A huge stone wall stretched for more than a mile along by this river and secluded paths wound in and out among the shady bushes.

Above me were the steep rocks covered with green shrubs. Now and then a sheep or a cow, separated from the herd, would come to the edge of the precipice and look down through the shrubbery.

When I came to Matlock I had just got to the description of Paradise in my reading of Milton's *Paradise Lost*, and the following lines, which I read in the ravine by the bank of the river, had a strong effect on my mind, for they describe the nature of the scene as clearly as if the poet had drawn on this very spot for his idea:

> ... delicious Paradise,
> Now nearer, crowns with her enclosure green,
> As with a rural mound, the champain head
> Of a steep wilderness, whose hairy sides
> With thicket overgrown, grotesque and wild,
> Access denied; ...*

From Matlock Bath a bridge gives access to the town of Matlock itself, which consists of no more than a few ramshackle houses and can hardly be called a village. There is a great deal of traffic here – on horseback and by carriages – because of the proximity of the baths.

From Matlock I went by way of several villages to a little town called Bakewell in a hilly and romantic countryside. Often I made my way by narrow mountain tracks at astonishing heights, seeing a few small cottages nestling deep down in the dale beneath. The grey stone walls that bounded the fields gave the whole district a wild aspect. The hills were mostly bare of trees and in the distance one could see herds feeding on their summits.

As I was passing through one village I heard a big country lad asking another if I was a Frenchman. It seemed he had been waiting a long time to see this wonder and his wish had now been gratified.

When I had passed through Bakewell, which is like Derby inasmuch as it is rather unimposing, my path ran by a fairly wide river and over a little mound where a cultivated field lay spread before me, making an indescribably gratifying impression on me. For this I could not account at once, but then I remembered that in my childhood I had seen a place almost identical to this near the village where I was brought up.

* Milton, *Paradise Lost*, Book IV, lines 132–7.

And although I was now in the middle of England the field was not enclosed by hedges, but open, as in Germany. It shone with an uninterrupted succession of greens and yellows – a most attractive colouring. This, and the thousand other small details of the scene which I can't enumerate, brought back to me the memory of my childhood.

I rested here, a mile outside Bakewell, and when I went on again I thought of my home in Germany, of all my acquaintances and of you, my friend. I thought if only you could see me wandering here! Then for the first time I thought of the distance between us; that I was now in England, a quite unthought-of place, and this notion came to me such as I have had only a few times in my life.

Was it the same with you, my friend, when we went on our journey to Hamburg and on the way from Perlberg visited your birthplace in the village of Boberow? Among the village folk you saw again your old schoolmates, and one who had become the village bailiff answered heartily when you asked him if he knew who you were: 'Why, yes! You're the Pastor's lad Fritz!' The schoolmaster answered with his stiff townee ceremony that he had not the honour of knowing you, as, during your presence there as a village child, he had not *in loco* been.

After my rest by the river I passed through another small place called Ashford. I wanted to reach a little village named Wardlow that evening and it lay only three miles away. But two men whom I had seen in Matlock came into view and shouted at me from a distance to wait for them. These were the first fellow-walkers who had offered to go along with me since I left Mr Modd in Oxford.

The first was a saddler who wore a short brown jacket, an apron and a round hat. The other was a very quiet man dressed like a simple townsman – quite unlike the talkative saddler.

I pricked up my ears as I heard the saddler begin to speak of Homer, Horace and Virgil. He quoted lines from their works, moreover, in a way I should have thought only possible in a doctor or master of arts from Oxford. He advised me not to stop at Wardlow, where I should find only mean accommodation, but to go on with him another couple of miles to Tideswell where he lived. This name 'Tideswell' he pronounced 'Tidsel', just as the common people of Birmingham call their town '*Brumidschäm*' ['Brummagem'].

We called at a little alehouse along the road where the saddler insisted on paying for my drink because he said he had taken me with him along the road.

Not far from this alehouse we came to a hill with a view which, my philosophic saddler said, may possibly be the only one of its kind in England. We saw beneath us a deep hollow, like a cauldron cut out of the surrounding earth, and at its foot a small valley containing a house beside a little stream meandering through a carpet of green pastureland. * The man who lived in this happy valley was a great naturalist who, following his bent as a scientist, had already transplanted there a great number of foreign plants. My escort expounded on the beauty of this valley in terms well-nigh poetical, while the third man, bored with his long harangue, grew resentful at the delay.

A steep path led us down into the valley. We passed through and emerged on the other side between the mountains.

Not far from Tideswell we lost our third companion, who lived thereabouts. Now we could see Tideswell before us in a valley, and the saddler began to tell me about his family, how he never quarrelled with his wife, had never threatened her with his fist nor said to her: 'Thou liest!'

* Monsal Dale.

At this point I must explain that it is taken as the grossest of insults if one man says to another 'Thou liest'. 'Thou'rt a liar' is still stronger and 'Thou'rt a damned liar' the very limit.

As in Germany nobody will tolerate the name of rogue or scoundrel, so in England the word 'liar' is the most offensive and can only be revenged by a fight.

Our Jacky in London looked at me wide-eyed when I said to him jokingly 'Thou'rt a liar', and I had much to do before he would make it up with me again.

If one can estimate the character of a nation from little things like this it seems to me that the general hatred of the word 'liar' is to the credit of the English.

With this observation I return to my saddler companion, who told me how he had to earn his bread away from home and was now for the first time in two months coming back to his family. Near the town he pointed out to me a row of trees which his father had planted and which he could not pass without emotion whenever he returned to his native place. His father had been a rich man but had used nearly all his means to support one son in America, leaving the other children poor. Nevertheless he respected his father and his heart was saddened whenever he saw those trees.

Tideswell consists of two rows of small houses built of undressed stone. On entering the place my guide drew my attention to the church — very handsome and in modern taste despite its antiquity.

He asked me whether he should take me to a high-class or a homely inn. I chose the latter and so he went with me to a small inn where he introduced me to the landlord as his travelling companion and a man of good perception.

They made their best endeavour to treat me as such, and prepared toasted cheese for me. This was Cheshire cheese toasted before the fire until it was melted. It is regarded as a right delicious dish, but unfortunately I couldn't eat any of it and invited my host to eat it. He enjoyed it as a rare treat. Then, as I drank neither brandy nor ale, he said I lived far too frugally for a walker, who must after all have enough strength to get along.

At this point I ought to mention that English innkeepers have plenty of opportunity for ale-drinking, and so those with a fondness for it grow astonishingly fat and round-faced. Much ale and brandy tippling makes a man quite bloated.

The following morning my landlady did me the honour of drinking coffee with me but stinted me of milk and sugar. It was Sunday and I went with my host to a barber on whose shop it said 'Shaving for a penny'. Many of the locals were assembled there and they took me for a gentleman because of my hat. I had bought it in London for a guinea and the quality of it filled them with wonder – a sign that luxury has not reached these parts.

In England as in Germany you will find stuck on doors inside a house cheap paper sheets bearing social maxims of the highest order, despite the shoddy material they are printed on. Some of these would do credit to the best moral authors. Here, in the barber's shop, I read among other things one which proclaimed a golden rule: 'Make no comparisons'. And when you think of the number of quarrels and disasters which arise in the world through setting one person's merits against another's there is in those few short words a valuable lesson in manners.

A man to whom I gave sixpence showed me the way out of the town and put me on the right road for Castleton. This road went along by a wall of piled-up stones such as I have already described. The whole district was rough and mountainous; the earth brought forth brown heather; here and there a sheep grazed. I made a short digression to a hill on the left, where I saw an awe-inspiring view of bare rocky mountains, beautiful in their way, stretching both near and far; the most distinguished bore black heather and presented a terrible aspect.

THIRTEEN

The Devil's Cavern

Castleton, June 30th (continued)

I HAD NOW LEFT LONDON a hundred and seventy miles
behind me. Ascending then one of the highest hills that I
had for some time seen before me I saw a thrilling sight. A
valley interwoven with rivulets and surrounded by a ring of
mountains lay spread out before me. In this valley lay
Castleton, a little town of simple houses taking its name
from an old castle, the ruins of which are still there to be
seen.

A narrow path winds down the side of the hill, which
led me through the valley and right into a Castleton street
where I found a hostelry and dined. Immediately I had done
this I set off for the cavern. A little brook which flows
through the town led me to its entrance.

For a while I stood staring in wonderment at the astound-
ing height of the cliff which rose before me. On both its
sides grew green bushes, while above it rose the crumbling
walls and towers of the old castle. Beneath me at the foot of

the cliff gaped the huge opening of the cave's entrance, pitch-dark as first seen in the glare of the midday sun.

As I stood wondering at all this I noticed a man in the gloomy entrance to the cave. His aspect was wild, and when he asked me if I wanted to see the cave his harsh voice echoed loudly from its depths.

I answered him in the affirmative, whereupon he asked me another question. Did I wish to be carried across the stream? He mentioned the fee for this. It was quite small.

His stringy black hair, dirty ragged clothes, his harsh voice and the question he asked were so fitting to the character of Charon that I could not shake off the uncanny feeling that the sight of this cave had begun to inspire.

As soon as I had agreed to his demand he told me to follow him fearlessly, and together we passed into the cave. In its entrance and on my left lay a huge tree-trunk on which the local boys were playing. Our path sloped gradually downwards and the daylight, entering only through the mouth of the cave, was left behind. We were enwrapped in twilight. And when we had gone a few steps forward, what a sight I saw! Glancing to my right I caught sight of a complete village under the huge wall of the cavern! As it was Sunday the inhabitants had a day off from their work and were sitting before their huts with their children. Hardly had we left these little dwellings behind us than I came upon a lot of big wheels, used by the subterranean villagers for the making of ropes. It was as if I were gazing upon the wheel of Ixion and the interminable labour of the Danaides.

As we went farther down into the cave the twilight deepened as the receding opening of the cave seemed to get smaller and smaller, until but a few rays of light reached us through the smoke that twisted up into the vault. This gradual closing in of darkness as you go down the steady incline inspires a soft melancholy; the thread of life is, as it were, being snipped off without any pain or grief and one wanders serenely to the peaceful land where there is no more care.

Finally the high arch of rock, which seemed to shut off heaven from the earth, was closed as we came to a small door where an old woman brought two candles, putting one into the hand of each of us. My guide now opened the door which cut us off from the last glimmer of daylight and led us into the temple of darkness. What we had previously passed through was the forecourt. The rock was now so low that for a few steps we had to stoop down in order to get through the passage; but consider my astonishment when we had done so, to find myself in a chamber so vast in every way – length, breadth and height – that the spacious opening forecourt through which we had passed was as nothing to it! Even in the dim light of our candles this was obvious.

After we had strolled about in here for a whole hour, beneath a roof as black as midnight, we came to a spot where the roof again sloped down low and suddenly we were on the bank of a broad river from whose waters our candles threw back most wonderful reflections.

A little boat had been beached here; it had some straw lying in it. My guide told me to get into the boat and stretch myself straight out in the bottom, because in the middle of the river the rocky roof descended so low that it almost touched the water.

When I had done this he jumped into the water up to his middle and drew the boat along after him.

Around us was a death-like stillness, and, as the boat went along, the roof of the cave sank ever lower, like a dark grey cloud, until it was nearly touching my face. I could hardly hold my candle upright before my breast and lay in my boat as in a coffin until we had passed this terrifying constriction, until the rock of the roof began to rise again and my guide set me ashore on the further bank.

Our road now varied – sometimes high and wide, at other times low and narrow. On both sides of us we saw many petrified plants and animals, great and small, but so numerous that we did not venture to examine them, for to do so would have taken several days. In this way we came to a second river, but it was not so wide as the first. The opposite bank could in fact be seen, but there was no boat; my guide took me on his shoulders and carried me across.

We went a few steps farther and came to a narrow watercourse stretching ahead into the distance, leading to the far end of the cave. The path we followed along its bank was wet and slippery and at times so narrow that we had difficulty in putting one foot before the other. But I was nevertheless walking contentedly along this underground shore, taking in the wonderful objects of interest in this kingdom of darkness and of shadow, when all at once I heard something sounding in my ears like far-off music.

Full of wonder I stood still. I asked my guide what it meant. All he would say was that I should soon see.

But as we went on again we lost the harmonious sound, the noise changed in character and merged into a gentle ripple like falling raindrops.

Then, to my great astonishment, rain suddenly began to fall from the rock above us, as though there were a dense raincloud there. The raindrops glistened in the light of our candles. This falling water was the cause of the melodious sound we had previously heard in the distance; it had penetrated the rock above and came upon us as a falling spray. We dared not go too near the falling drops with our lights for fear they should be extinguished and we ourselves unable to find our way back in the darkness.

So we went along by the narrow strip of water, often catching glimpses of other deep openings in the walls on either side of our track which were the entrances to yet more caves. All these we passed by. Then my guide told me to get ready for one of the most marvellous spectacles we should see. And hardly had we gone more than a few more steps than we emerged into a majestic temple with a magnificent arch supported by beautiful pillars such as could only have been designed by the most refined of craftsmen.

This subterranean temple seemed to me in that moment to surpass all the most famous buildings in form, beauty and splendour, yet no hand of man had touched it. Filled with adoration, I saw here the majesty of the Creator revealed in the innermost depths of Nature. In this solemn silence and in this holy darkness I offered up a prayer before I left the temple.

We were now nearing the end of our journey.

Our trusted watercourse led us through the remaining part of the cavern to where the vaulted rock makes its final arch and again dips low to mingle with the flood, which here forms a small half-circle and so closes the cavern that no mortal can go a step farther.

My guide sprang in, swam a few strokes under water beneath the rock and returned dripping wet to demonstrate to me that this was the end of the cavern, unless, at some time, the rock should be blasted with gunpowder and a second cave opened up.

Naturally I now thought that there was nothing more to do but make our way back. It proved, however, that there were still more strenuous efforts to be made and still more beautiful things to be seen.

As we returned, my guide went to the left and I followed him through an opening in the high wall of rock. He asked me if I could bring myself to crawl for some distance under a low rock – a rock so low that it nearly touched the surface of the ground. As I replied in the affirmative he told me to follow him, but warned me to take care of my light.

So we went on all fours through the wet sand, through an opening in the rocks so narrow that at times it was no more than just wide enough to allow my body to wriggle through.

This operation over, I saw in the cave a stone hill so high that it seemed to be lost in the highest rocks as in a cloud. The hill was so wet and slippery that I slid back when I tried to ascend. However, my guide took me by the hand and told me I had only to follow him confidently because he knew the foot-holds.

We mounted this slippery hill. On both sides were such precipices that I still feel giddy whenever I think of them.

We arrived at last on the summit, where the hill lost itself in the rock. My guide placed me on a spot where I could stand firmly and told me to stay there, keeping absolutely still. Then he went down the hill again with his light, leaving me quite alone.

For a long time I lost sight of him. Then he reappeared – or at least his light did – shining up like a beautiful star from the depths of the chasm.

After I had enjoyed this beautiful sight for some time, my guide returned, took me on his shoulders and merrily bore me down the slippery hill. Then he went up again, leaving me now in the depths, and while I shielded my light with my hand he let his light shine down from a little opening in the rock. Its gleam surpassed in beauty all that I had seen.

Our trip was now accomplished and we returned through our narrow passage with much fatigue and difficulty. We saw anew the temple we had left a short time before, we heard again the rainfall, pattering down when we were near but blending into a musical sound when we heard it afar off. We crossed the silent rivers and the wide expanse of the first great chamber, back to the little narrow door where we had last seen the light of day, to greet it again after being for so long in the dark.

But before my guide opened this he said: 'Now I will show you a sight surpassing far in beauty all I have shown you yet.' And I found that he was right, for when he had opened the door only halfway, the sight of things seen in the reappearing twilight was like a glimpse of Elysium.

It was as if night and the gloom were being dispersed by a slowly dawning day. In the distance I saw once more the smoke from the huts, then the huts themselves, and as we mounted higher I saw the boys still playing round their huge tree-trunk; until at last the sky – rosy and purple-striped – could be seen through the mouth of the cave, and as we emerged the sun sank in the west.

I had thus spent the whole afternoon in that cavern. My clothes were now in much the same state as my guide's and my shoes would hardly cling to my feet, so soaked and torn were they from going through the damp sand and over the hard sharp stones.

I paid only half-a-crown for being conducted on this adventure, and I gave a tip to my guide; because he received none of the official fee, but had to hand it all over to his master, who lived very comfortably on the income from this cavern, keeping an underling to show the people round.

FOURTEEN
More of the Midlands

Castleton, June 30th (continued)

WHEN I ARRIVED home I sent at once for a shoemaker. He lived right opposite and came to examine my shoes. These caused him much surprise; it seemed incredible to him that I should have come all the way from Germany wearing shoes so badly made. But since he had no new pair on hand he undertook to improve mine as much as possible.

I struck up a friendship with this shoemaker and when I told him about my exploring the cave he seemed delighted that there should be something in this little town to bring wonderment to people from far-off lands. He offered to take me for a short walk and show me the famous mountain called Mam Tor, one of the wonders of Nature in Derbyshire.

This mountain is covered with turf on its back and sides, but at one end forms a steep precipice. The body of this mountain, however, is not of hard rock like the other mountains, but consists of loose earth [shale] which breaks away and either trickles downward in small quantities or collapses in great lumps which roll down with a noise like thunder. These fallen quantities of earth pile up at the foot of the mountain and in this way are building up a smaller hill which continually grows higher.

It seems probable that the name of this mountain – Mam Tor – comes from this phenomenon and means 'Mother tor' [or mountain]; for 'tor' is an abbreviation of 'tower', meaning the height, while 'mam' is a common abbreviation of 'mother'. The mountain is creating the hill at its foot and is therefore its mother. There is a belief among the local inhabitants that the mountain still remains the same size notwithstanding the daily loss of material from its body. *

My guide told me a terrifying story of a Castleton man who made a bet that he would climb the loose precipice of Mam Tor.

So long as he was on the lower slopes, where the gradient is fairly gentle, he could get a good hold with his feet in the loose shale and he clambered up without a look behind. But after he had climbed something over halfway up and had arrived at the point where the precipice overhung its basis he glanced down, unlucky man, while the unstable mass of the point of the precipice reared above him.

He began to tremble all over; his hands and feet were failing to retain their hold and he dared not venture to go either up or down. So he remained for a time between heaven and earth, his mind turning desperately round the thought of his predicament. Then, when his sinews could hold the strain no longer, he braced himself for an effort, and, clawing at one loose stone after another – any one of which would have let him down had he not immediately

* Mam Tor: the Shivering Mountain.

grabbed at another – he scrambled with luck to the top, cheating an almost certain death, to his own surprise and that of the onlookers.

He won his bet.

I shuddered as I heard this story, seeing in my mind the man scrambling up that precipice right near to me.

Not far from this point is the Eldon Hole – a hole in the ground of such enormous depth that if you throw a pebble down it and lay your ear to the ground at its rim you can hear the pebble falling for a long time. All the time it is falling you hear remarkable sounds. First, with the release of the pebble, a sound like a sigh, then, as the pebble strikes against the hard sides of the hole on its descent, oscillating to and fro, a rumble like subterranean thunder, until, after a long time falling it reaches the bottom and the noise suddenly ends in a hiss.

The credulous folk hereabouts firmly believe that one of them once threw a goose into this hole and that it reappeared two miles away in the Great Peak Cavern I have described, completely featherless. They believe other fairy-tales of the same order.

In Derbyshire they tell of the Seven Wonders of Nature, of which this Eldon Hole is one; another is Mam Tor and a third the Great Peak Cavern which goes locally by the rather dirty name of 'The Devil's Arse'.

The remaining four Wonders of Nature are Poole's Cavern [at Buxton] which has some resemblance to the Great Peak Cavern although I have not seen it; St Ann's Well [also at Buxton] where two springs emerge quite close to each other, one boiling hot and the other ice-cold. * Next wonder is a spring not far from Tideswell – the village

* Moritz is misinformed. The constant temperature of the water is 82° F. 500,000 gals per day.

through which I passed – this is called the Tides' Well*
because for most of the time the water flows almost un-
noticed and then, all at once, makes a mighty rumbling but
not unmusical noise as it gushes up and overflows its banks.
The last of the Seven Wonders is Chatsworth, a mansion at
the foot of a snow-covered mountain. While this suggests
most dismal winter, at its foot blooms pleasant spring. I can
tell you no more about these last four Wonders, however,
because I only know them from hearsay. I was told about
them by my shoemaker guide during our walk.

While he was showing me round and hazarding on the
sort of wonderful things I had seen on the travels far and
wide I had already undertaken, he grew excited at the
thought of them and wanted keenly to travel himself; I had
enough to do to make him reconsider his desire. All evening
he couldn't stop talking about it and declared that if he had
not got a wife and child he would have set forth next day,
for there was little work to be had in Castleton and only a
mean living to be made. And he was not yet thirty years old!

On our way back he wanted to show me the lead mines,
only it was too late. Yet he repaired my shoes that evening
with the skill of a master craftsman.

I have brought with me from the cave a cough which I
don't like at all. It gives me much pain and I think one is
forced to breathe damp air in that cavern; but in that case
how has Charon stuck it so long?

This morning I rose early in order to see the ruined
castle and to climb the very high hill adjacent.

The ruins stand right over the mouth of the cave, on a
hill which extends well beyond the ruins, getting ever
broader, but in the front it is so narrow that the castle wall
occupies all this part of the hill. Downwards from the castle

* More commonly 'the ebbing and flowing well'

it is all steep rock, so there is no access to it from the town except by a path hewn out of the rock, and that is very steep.

The ruins stand on a spot all overgrown with nettles and thistles. Formerly there would be a bridge joining one cliff with another opposite; some traces remain, for in the valley beneath can be found the remains of the arch which once supported the bridge. This valley, which lies behind the ruins and probably over the Great Peak Cavern, is called the Caves Way and is one of the main roads to the town. It begins very gently in the distance and descends between the two mountains on a course by no means tiring, but if you miss this course and continue over the hill, you will be in great danger of falling from the cliff as it gets steeper all the time.

The mountain on which the ruins stand is completely rocky, but the other – on the left of it across the vale – is grass-grown, with the pastures on its summit separated by undressed stone walls. This green hill is at least three times as high as that on which the ruins stand.

I started to climb the green hill. This is also rather steep and when I had got just over halfway up without looking round I found myself in much the same situation as the man who had climbed Mam Tor for a wager. I found on looking back that I had no head for heights; the sight of the land lying like a map beneath me almost unnerved me; the roofs of the houses seemed to be almost on the ground and the castle mound itself lay at my feet.

I grew giddy at this sight and had to use all my reason to prove to myself that I was in no danger; in any case I could scramble down the green turf in the same way as I had come up it. But in time I grew accustomed to the view until at last it gave me real satisfaction. I climbed to the summit, walked across the pastures and came at last to the road which brought me gently through the valley between the two mountains.

Above me in the pasture on the mountain some milk-maids had been milking their cows and were now returning down this road with their milking-pails on their heads. It was beautiful to see a group of these girls, taking shelter beneath an overhanging rock, chatting confidentially to each other as they sat on natural seats formed by the stones.

My road brought me back into the town, from where I am now writing to you. Soon I shall be leaving to start my journey back to London. I shall not, however, go back by exactly the same route.

Northampton, July [*5th*]

When I took leave of my shoemaker in Castleton, who would so dearly have liked to come with me, I resolved not to return by way of Tideswell but by Wardlow, which is shorter.

There I found a single inn attended only by the house-wife, who told me that her husband worked in the lead mines and that the cave I had visited in Castleton, and everything else I had seen, were as nothing in comparison. Her husband could show me round them.

When I wanted to pay for my lunch she objected that I had drunk no ale or brandy, on which she generally made her profit, and so she couldn't rightly make me out a bill. So I let her serve me with a pot of ale without me drinking it, so as to make her account correct.

While in this inn I saw again my landlord from Tides-well; he didn't travel on foot like me but came riding proudly on a horse.

I went on my way, the mountains familiar to me from

my journey northwards rising before me. Then I read in Milton, straight away, the scene of the Creation, where the angel describes to Adam how the waters sank and the bare mountains heaved up their broad backs:

> Immediately the mountains huge appear
> Emergent, and their broad, bare backs upheave
> Into the clouds, their tops ascend the sky.

Reading this passage it seemed to me that everything around me was, as it were, in the beginning; so vivid was the image that the mountains seemed indeed to heave themselves up before my eyes. I had felt something like this on my journey outwards when sitting right opposite to a mountain whose tip was covered with trees. So doing I read in Milton the description of the battle of the angels, where the fallen ones assail their antagonists with a terrific bombardment and they in turn defend themselves by each seizing a mountain by its tree-tufted tip, tearing the hill out by its foundation and so, bearing their hills in their hands, advance upon the fiends:

> ... They ran, they flew
> From their foundations loos'ning to and fro
> They plucked the seated hills with all their load.
> Rocks, waters, woods, and by the shaggy tops
> Uplifting bore them in their hands.

I imagined I saw the angel stand and shake in the air the mountain that lay before me.

In the evening when it was already dark I came to the last village before Matlock and decided to stay at the inn which a man told me was at the end of the village. But I went on nearly until midnight before I came to the end of that village. It seemed it would have no end. On my journey out I must either not have passed through this village or I had not noticed its length.

Tired and not a little ill I came at last to the inn, sat myself by the fire in the kitchen and asked for something to eat. As they told me I could not have a bed, I insisted that I positively would not be driven away, but would spend the night sitting by the fire. There I remained, laying my head on the table in order to sleep.

When they thought I was asleep I heard them talking about me, trying to make out what sort of man I could be. A woman took my part, saying: 'I dare say he is a well-bred gentleman.' Another contradicted her because I had come on foot, and said: 'He is a poor travelling creature.'

My ears still tingle when I think of the way she said 'Poor travelling creature'. In a few short words it forced upon me the disdain they had for an outcast – all the tragedy of a man with no native place.

At last, when they saw that I still remained there, they gave me a bed, just as I had given up all hope of getting one; and when they asked me for a shilling next morning I gave them half-a-crown and would not take the change, just to reverse the sting of that phrase, 'Poor travelling creature'. They treated me after that very politely and apologetically, and I went away contented.

When I had passed through Matlock I did not go to Derby again but turned left for Nottingham; the mountains were left behind and my road took me again over the fields.

At this stage I must remind you that the word 'peak' generally means the tip of a mountain, but 'The Peak' or 'High Peak' of Derbyshire, as many say, is the mountainous or highest part of that county.

Towards midday I came again to a hill on which there was a remarkable inn sign bearing a motto in rhyme, ending with the words 'Refresh and then go on'. Above the sign I read the phrase 'Entertainment for horse and man'. This I have seen on other inn signs. But the commonest inscription on the signs of small inns is 'Dealer in foreign liquors'.

I lunched here on a piece of cold meat and salad. Either these or eggs and salad were my usual midday and evening meals in the inns where I stayed. I seldom got anything warm. They gave me the ingredients for the salad but I had always to mix them myself, as is the custom here.

The going was fairly pleasant but the countryside lacked variety. Nevertheless it was a beautiful evening, and as I passed through a village shortly before sundown I was greeted by various people with the words, 'Fine night' or 'Fine evening'. Some greeted me with 'How do you do?' to which the answer is 'I thank you'. This form of greeting must seem very unusual to a foreigner, coming from a man he has never seen before in his life and asking all at once what he does, or how he finds himself!

After I had gone through the village I arrived at a green with an inn on the far side. The landlady sat at the window. I asked her if I could stay the night; she said 'No!' and slammed the window in my face.

It recalled to my mind all the similar experiences I had met with in this country and I couldn't help voicing my resentment at the inhospitality of the English. As I walked on, however, I reconsidered my judgment as I remembered the occasions when I had been well received.

Still early enough I came to another inn with the sign of Navigation Inn, so called because the coal-bargees on the River Trent rest here after their work.

A wilder, coarser type of men than those I met gathered

together in the kitchen of this inn I have never seen, and in their company I was obliged to spend the evening.

Their speech, their clothing, their appearance – all were rough and their language even more dreadful. Hardly a word came out of their mouths without a 'God damn me!' to it; and so, with blaspheming, brawling and cursing, the time went on. But I did nothing for them to complain of; on the contrary they drank my health and I was careful to drink theirs as I remembered my brush with the landlord of the inn at Matlock. So every time I drank I said: 'Your health, gentlemen all!'

When two Englishmen quarrel, actions mean more than words. They say little but repetitions of the same thing, clinching it with a hearty 'God damn you!' Their anger boils up inside them and soon breaks out in violence.

The hostess, who sat in the kitchen with this company, was nevertheless well dressed and inclined to put on airs.

After I had supped I hurried off to bed, but my sleep was disturbed by the bargees roaring and raving nearly all the night. But when I got up in the morning there was not one of them to be seen or heard.

I had now only a few miles to go to Nottingham, which I reached at midday.

Of all the towns I have seen outside London, Nottingham is the loveliest and neatest. Everything had a modern look, and a large space in the centre was hardly less handsome than a London square. A charming footpath leads over the fields to the highway, where a bridge spans the Trent. Not far from this bridge was an inn where I ate my midday meal. I could get nothing but bread and butter so I asked them to make it into toast.

Nottingham stands on a hill, and, with its high houses,

red roofs and church steeples, looks excellent from a distance. At no town in England have I enjoyed so beautiful a prospect.

Then I passed through a number of villages — Ruddington, Bradmore, Bunny and Costock where I spent the night. All that afternoon I heard bells ringing in the villages, which possibly meant that they were keeping a holiday. The sky was overcast and I felt somewhat ill; this bell-ringing made me even more heavy-minded and melancholy.

There were three inns adjacent to each other in Costock, which, to judge by their exteriors, were dens of the most abject poverty. At the one where I stayed only the landlady was at home. A sick carter and a sick butcher were staying there for the night, which depressed me. During the evening I felt a kind of fever, slept disturbed that night and lay in bed very long the next morning until my landlady woke me, saying she was getting worried on my account. I decided to travel on beyond Leicester by coach.

I was now only four miles from Loughborough, an unseemly small town where I arrived late in the middle of the day and ordered a meal at the last inn on the way to Leicester. They received me at once as a gentleman — rather unexpectedly — and allowed me to sit in the parlour.

From Loughborough to Leicester is only ten miles but the road is sandy and hard going. I passed through a place called Mountsorrel, which probably gets its name from a small hill at one end; the rest of the way to Leicester is one great flat plain.

Towards evening I arrived in Leicester through a pleasant meadow by way of a footpath; lying lengthways before me Leicester looked well, and bigger than it really is.

I walked down a long street until I came to the inn from which the coaches start. Here I learned that another stage-coach for London would leave that evening, but all the inside seats were booked. But there was still room on the outside. Time was short, however, if I was to reach London in time to keep my appointment with the Hamburg sea-captain who had agreed to take me to Germany. I therefore booked a place on the outside of the coach as far as Northampton.

That journey from Leicester to Northampton I shall remember as long as I live.

The coach started from the courtyard of the inn. The inside passengers got in there, but the roof of the archway leading from the courtyard to the street was too low to permit passengers to be on the top of the coach without danger to their heads, so we 'outsiders' had to clamber up in the street.

My travelling companions on top of the coach were a farmer, a young man quite decently dressed, and a young Negro. Climbing up was in itself at the risk of life and when I got on top I made straight for a corner where I could sit and take hold of a little handle on the side of the coach. I sat over the wheel and imagined I saw certain death before my eyes as soon as we set off. All I could do was to take a firmer grip of the handle and keep my balance.

The coach rolled along the stony street at great speed and every now and then we were tossed into the air; it was a near wonder that I always landed back on the coach. This sort of thing happened whenever we went through a village or down a hill.

Being continually in fear of my life finally became intolerable. I waited until we were going comparatively slowly and then crept from the top of the coach into the luggage-basket behind.

'In the basket you will be shaken to death!' exclaimed the Negro.

And I took it for a mere figure of speech!

Going uphill everything was comfortable and I nearly went to sleep between the travelling-boxes and the parcels, but as soon as we started to go downhill all the heavy luggage began to jump about. Everything came alive! I got so many hard knocks from them at every moment that I thought my end had come. Now I knew that the negro had uttered no mere figure of speech. My cries for help were of no avail. I had to suffer this buffeting for nearly an hour until we began to go uphill again and, badly bruised and shaken, I crept back on to the roof of the coach and took up my former position.

'Didn't I tell you you would be shaken to death?' asked the Negro as I crawled back. I kept silent.

I am writing this as a warning to anyone who should unwittingly think of riding on the outside of an English stage-coach – or even in the basket!

We arrived about midnight in Market Harborough, where I was able to rest a little before being driven at full speed through many villages to arrive some time before dawn in Northampton, thirty-three miles from Leicester.

I had an equally fearful ride from Market Harborough to Northampton. It rained nearly all the time, and so we who were on the outside of the coach and had already been covered with dust, were now drenched as well. My neighbour, the young man, who sat with me in the middle, slept occasionally and in doing so fell against me with the full weight of his body, so that I feared he would push me right off my seat.

At last we came to Northampton where I went straight to bed and have slept nearly until noon. Early in the morning I propose to take the coach for London.

FIFTEEN

The return to London

London, July 14th

I CANNOT CALL the passage from Northampton to London a ride so much as a shift from place to place in a shut-up box. When you travel in this way you may find yourself in the company of a few people with whom you can talk – if you are lucky.

My luck was out. My companions were tenant farmers who slept so soundly that even their hearty manner of greeting couldn't disturb them. Their faces, bloated with beer and brandy, lay before me like fat lumps of dead flesh, and when they awoke they talked only of their trade – sheep!

The third occupant of the coach was very different from the other two. His face was sallow and haggard, his eyes deep-sunk and his long yellow fingers shook. The man looked mean and misanthropic.

Mean he certainly was. Whenever we came to a posting station where it was customary to tip the coachman he gave nothing, although the rest of us gave something; and every time he had to pay anything it forced a 'God damn' from his heart.

He seemed to shun the light as he sat in the coach, and, so far as he was able, kept all the windows shut. So they would have remained had I not occasionally opened one in order to catch a glimpse of the passing scenery.

We went by way of Newport Pagnell, Dunstable, St Albans and Barnet to Islington, where we entered London itself; but the names are all I know of these places.

In Dunstable I think it was we breakfasted, and the custom proved to be the same here as in Germany; all the passengers paid equal shares of the whole bill. I did not know this was the custom and had ordered coffee specially for myself; but it was all right because the three farmers drank some of my coffee and I drank some of their tea.

They asked me from what part of the world I came, whereas we Germans ask what country a man belongs to.

After we had breakfasted, the farmers regained their normal spirits – except the thin one – and began a discussion on religion and politics.

One of them brought the story of Samson on the carpet. His local parson had recently explained this, but he had all sorts of doubt about the great gates which Samson carried away and the foxes with the firebrands between their tails, although he was firm in his faith.

They told each other all sorts of stories from the Bible – not as if they propounded a truth, but simply as good stories which they had heard. For the most part they had heard them from the parson and not read them personally. One started on about the Jews in the Old Testament and maintained that the present race of Jews sprang from them.

Said the other: 'They are eternally damned,' as cold-blooded and certain of himself as if he already saw them burning.

Fresh passengers now joined us frequently, but only for short distances, after which they got out. Among them was a woman brandy-distiller from London, who held our attention with a detailed account of the alarming events of the recent [Gordon] riots. I was particularly struck with the story of how a fellow opposite to her house became so enraged that he stood on the wall of a house already half burnt down and tried with his own bare hands to tear down the stones the fire had spared, until he was shot and fell back among the flames.

About one o'clock we arrived safely in a London teeming with rain. I had had to pay sixteen shillings in advance at Northampton for the sixty-six-mile journey and the coachman seemed uncertain about this. Anyway, when he asked me if I had paid, he had to take my word for it.

I looked dishevelled when I arrived in London; nevertheless Mr Pointer – with whom you will remember I had left my trunk – received me with great friendliness and listened over the table to my story of adventures.

In the evening I visited Herr Leonhardi, who got me into the Freemasons' Tavern because I did not want to rent lodgings during the few days I should have to wait for a fair wind. But I have now waited eight days in the Freemasons' Tavern and the wind still remains contrary. I ardently wish it would veer right for Hamburg, for I dare not go far away from here in case it does; I must be ready to board the ship as soon as the wind turns favourable.

Rockingham's death and the consequent change of ministry are all the news now. Everyone is put out over Fox's resignation and yet the remarkable thing is that they all interest themselves personally in him as in one of whom they are sorry to have to disapprove.

On Tuesday there was a most important debate in Parliament. Fox was called on to explain to the country the reasons for his resignation. At eleven in the morning the gallery was so full that not another seat was to be had, yet the debates do not start until three in the afternoon, going on until ten at night.

Fox arrived about four. Everybody was brimming with expectation. He spoke with great vehemence at first, but it was noted that he toned down as he went on, and when he had defended all his motives, step by step, he ended by saying: 'Now I stand here again, poor as I was,' etc. The scene was deeply touching. All who listened were deeply impressed.

General Conway then gave his grounds for not resigning, although he was of the same opinion as Mr Fox and Mr Burke regarding the independence of America, the Irish regulations and an improvement in the representation of the English people in Parliament; he did not think, however, that the present minister, Lord Shelburne, would act against these principles. If he should do so General Conway said he would resign at once, but not before.

Then Burke rose to make a flowery speech in praise of the late Marquis of Rockingham. In the course of it he found that some members were not listening and that a good deal of private chatter was audible. 'This is no way to treat a member of such long standing as mine!' he declared forcibly and in a voice charged with emotion: 'I will be heard!' And at once they all became quiet.

After Burke had said a great deal in praise of Rockingham he turned to comment on General Conway's reason for wishing to remain in the ministry. He said it reminded him of a fable he had heard in childhood, how a wolf in sheep's clothing was led into the fold by a lamb. The lamb felt obliged to ask, 'Mama, why have you got such long claws and sharp teeth?' but nevertheless let him in. The wolf slaughtered the whole herd. Now, with regard to General Conway, it was as if the lamb noticed the claws and teeth but thought all the same that the wolf would change his nature and become a lamb. By this he said he wished to cast no reflection on Lord Shelburne, only this much he did know – that the present administration was a thousand times worse than it had been under Lord North.

Lord North sat among them.

When I first heard Mr Pitt speak I was astonished to see such a young man stand up in Parliament, and that his speech should attract so much attention. He seemed no more than a young man of twenty-one – yet this same Pitt is a minister and has now been made Chancellor of the Exchequer.

Twelve or more newspapers are brought out daily in London – some siding with the Government, some with the Opposition. It is shocking how they seize every opportunity for personal abuse. Only yesterday it was stated that after his fall from office in favour of the youthful Pitt, Fox re-marked, 'O hateful sight!' – as Satan did in *Paradise Lost* when he looked upon the being God approved – man!

On Thursday the King prorogued Parliament for the Long Vacation, but this has been written about enough already, so I shall pass it over.

I have also recently got to know the famous walker, Baron Grothaus, to whom Baron Groote of Hamburg wrote me an invitation. He lives in Chesterfield House, not far from General Paoli, to whom he has promised to introduce me when I have time for a visit.

For the rest, I have suffered much from the bad cough I caught in the Devil's Cavern, and for a few days I have not dared to go out. But Herr Schönborn and Herr Leonhardi have visited me assiduously and done much to cheer me up.

I have said as much about my travels outside London as I shall probably have to say about all England when I get back to Germany. Most of the people here in London to whom I speak about my travels tell me that what I have seen is quite new to them.

I think I ought to tell you what I have come to think about English declamation, pronunciation and dialect. I have forgotten to mention this subject previously.

English declamation seems to have not anything like so many variations as ours. In parliamentary addresses, sermons, theatrical speeches and even in common life the final periods are always spoken with a fall of the voice, singularly uniform, but which, for all its monotony, has something in it solid and impressive, so that a foreigner learns to imitate it with difficulty. Herr Leonhardi seemed to me, from a few lines he quoted from *Hamlet*, to have acquired this fall of voice very well. Moreover, the emphasis is placed rather more on the epithet than on the substantive, which they often allow to sink in favour of its adjective. In the theatre they emphasize the syllables and words very clearly, so that one can learn most about English oratory by listening to the actors.

London also has its special dialect. For example, they say, 'It a'nt' instead of 'It is not', 'I do' know' for 'I do not know', or 'I don't know'. 'I do' know him' means 'I don't know him'. This last has often confused me, causing me to take a negative for an affirmative.

The word 'sir' has innumerable uses in English. With the word 'sir' an Englishman addresses his king, his friend, his foe, his servant and his dog. He uses it to ask a polite question and a speaker in Parliament makes a stop-gap of it when he doesn't know what to say next.

Spoken as a question, 'Sir?' means 'What do you wish?' 'Sir!' in a threatening tone means: 'A box on the ear is at your service.' Said to a dog it proclaims a sound thrashing, and in a parliamentary speech, accompanied by a pause, it means: 'I can't think of what comes now.'

Nothing is oftener heard than the phrase: 'Never mind it!' meaning 'Let it alone!' A porter fell and struck his head on the pavement. 'Never mind it,' said a passer-by. When my trunk was being lifted off the ship into a boat the helmsman steered in between two other boats, and his lad, standing in the bows, got a good hiding because the others couldn't get through. 'Never mind it!' said the old man and kept on the same course.

Germans who have been here a long while speak German in almost pure Anglicisms, such as: 'Es will nicht tun' instead of 'Es ist nicht hinlänglich' and the like. In fact some even say: 'Ich habe es nicht *geminded*' for 'Ich habe mich nicht daran erinnert' or 'daran gedacht'. *

You can soon tell an Englishman who speaks German by the way he pronounces 'w' in the English manner. Instead of 'Ich befinde mich wohl' they say 'Ich befinde mich u-ohl' with the 'w' almost as weak as a quickly-spoken 'u'.

When someone is being shown the way I have often heard a kind of stock phrase: 'Go down the street as far as you can and then ask anybody,' just as we should say: 'Any child can direct you there.'

I have already told you that they learn to write a finer hand in England than we do. This may be because in the whole of England only one style of handwriting is admissible,

* All this is antiquated German anyway. (Translator)

in which the lettering is so clear that you might take it for print.

In general the arts of speaking, handwriting, expression and literary style seem to be further decided than among us Germans. The commonest man expresses himself in the proper phrases and anyone who writes a book at least writes correctly, even if the matter is poor. Good style seems to have spread all over England.

I have heard the most miserable twaddle from the pulpits. Today I have been in several churches where the sermons seemed to have been drawn from pamphlets on dogma. It is said there is a Jew living here from whom the clergy order sermons to be written for money.

SIXTEEN

Farewell

TODAY I AM WRITING to you from London for the last time, and in London from St Katherine's – the filthiest hole in the town. But here I must stay because this is where the big ships berth on the Thames and we sail as soon as the wind turns. It has in fact already turned, but we don't sail until tomorrow, so today I can again recount to you all that I know.

On Monday morning I moved from the Freemasons' Tavern to an inn here kept by a German landlord and patronized by all the Hamburg sea-captains. My bill for eight days in the Freemasons' Tavern came to one guinea, nine shillings and ninepence for lodging, breakfast and mid-day dinner. Breakfast, dinner and coffee were charged at one shilling each indiscriminately, while for lodging I paid no more than twelve shillings a week, which is undoubtedly very cheap.

Everything is cheap too at the German's in St Katherine's. You can eat, drink and lodge here for half-a-guinea a week, but I would not advise anyone to live here who wants to see

London, for St Katherine's is one of the most out-of-the-way and inconvenient places in the town.

Anyone who lands here, seeing these miserable dirty streets, and these houses all threatening to collapse, gets an impression of London quite unworthy of that magnificent and renowned city.

From Bulstrode Street or Cavendish Square to St Katherine's is well-nigh half a day's journey; nevertheless Herr Schönborn has visited me daily since I have been here, and I have walked halfway back with him. This afternoon we took leave of each other beside St Paul's Cathedral. I went away with a very heavy heart.

This afternoon, too, I received a most acceptable visit from Herr Hansen, an assistant working on the *Zöllnerschen Lesebuch für alle Stände* (Reading-book for all classes), who brought me a letter from Pastor Zöllner of Berlin.[*] Herr Hansen has just arrived in London as I am on the point of leaving, and is going to Liverpool on business.

During the last few days I have been through some London districts merely in order to kill time. Yesterday I tried to reach the West End, only it is a long way off – one house after another, everlastingly making up a street – until it grew dark and I returned tired out without having reached my goal.

Nothing in London makes a more detestable sight than the butchers' stalls, especially in the neighbourhood of the Tower. The guts and other refuse are all thrown on the street and set up an unbearable stink.

I have forgotten to tell you anything about the Royal Exchange. This imposing building is shaped like a long quadrangle with an open-air space in the middle where the merchants assemble. Round it are covered passages with the

* Johann Friedrich Zöllner (1753–1804).

names of the countries with which one may wish to do business always indicated on the pillars. There are also stone seats placed under the roofed passages, very convenient for a rest after walking from somewhere like St Katherine's.

Round about the walls are stuck advertisements printed on large sheets, on one of which I read a most remarkable screed. An English clergyman pleaded for men not to assent to the infamous parliamentary Bill for toleration of Roman Catholics, nor to allow any child to be led to everlasting ruin by their teaching and method of upbringing: rather that they should hand them over to the profit of some right-thinking priest of the Church of England.

In the middle of the open space stands a statue of Charles II. I realized as I sat on a bench to watch the bustling crowd, how little difference in dress and outward appearance there is between this London world and ours in Berlin.

Close to the Royal Exchange is a little shop where you can read as many of the current newspapers as you wish on payment of a penny or a halfpenny. This shop is continuously full; people stand and read hastily for a while, pay their halfpenny and go.

There is a little tower on the Royal Exchange which contains a chime of bells. These ring very pleasantly but not more than one rather merry tune sounds in the ears. *

Further, it occurs to me that there is no need for elementary primers and prints for the education of children: you can take them about the streets and show them all the things themselves. For in London care is taken to show, as far as practicable, all works of art and industry to the public. Paintings, machines, precious objects – all can be seen advantageously displayed behind great clear-glass windows. There is no lack of onlookers standing stock-still in the middle

* The carillon has now a considerable repertory.

of the street here and there to admire some ingenious novelty. Such a street often resembles a well-arranged show-cabinet.

But the squares where the graceful houses are, scorn this showing-off. It is suitable only for tradesmen's premises. The squares too are not so populous as the other parts of the city. The relationship of the Strand to the squares in bustle and business can be compared with that between the Mühlendamm and Friedrichstadt in Berlin.

And now, my friend, I cannot think of anything more to write to you about. Nothing worthwhile, I mean, except that all is ready for our departure tomorrow. I had to pay four guineas for food and lodging in the cabin to Captain Hilkes, with whom I sailed from Hamburg, but Captain Braunschweig, with whom I am to return, takes five guineas because the cost of provisions is dear in London.

And now I have told you all my destiny and all my adventures from the moment when I parted from you on the street in Hamburg, except of my voyage to London with Captain Hilkes. All I need tell you of that is – it lasted fourteen days, to my extreme discomfort, and that I was seasick for three of them. I shall bring you news in person of my return journey. Remember me to Biester,* and farewell until we meet again.

* J. E. Biester (1749–1816).

OTHER BOOKS BY
CARL PHILIP MORITZ

In addition to *Reisen eines Deutschen in England im Jahr 1782*, Moritz wrote another travel book: *Reisen eines Deutschen in Italien in den Jahren 1786–88*. In Rome he met Goethe, who later used Moritz's *Versuch einer deutschen Prosodie* (1786) when deciding the verse-form of *Iphigenie*. Moritz also wrote a little book on aesthetics entitled *Über die bildende Nachahmung des Schönen* (1788), and *Die Götterlehre* (1791). He is best remembered in his own country, however, for his psychological novels, *Andreas Hartknopf* (1786) and *Anton Reiser* (1785–90).

INDEX

Previously published by
ELAND BOOKS

MEMOIRS OF A
BENGAL CIVILIAN

JOHN BEAMES
**The lively narrative of a Victorian
district-officer**

With an introduction by Philip Mason

They are as entertaining as Hickey . . . accounts like these illuminate the dark corners of history.
Times Literary Supplement

John Beames writes a splendidly virile English and he is incapable of being dull; also he never hesitates to speak his mind. It is extraordinary that these memoirs should have remained so long unpublished . . . the discovery is a real find.
John Morris, The Listener

A gem of the first water. Beames, in addition to being a first-class descriptive writer in the plain Defoesque manner, was that thing most necessary of all in an autobiographer – an original. His book is of the highest value.
The Times

*If you wish to receive details of forthcoming publications,
please send your address to
Eland Books, 53 Eland Road, London SW11 5JX*

A VISIT TO DON OTAVIO

SYBILLE BEDFORD
A Mexican Journey

I am convinced that, once this wonderful book
becomes better known, it will seem incredible that it
could ever have gone out of print.
Bruce Chatwin, Vogue

This book can be recommended as vastly enjoyable.
Here is a book radiant with comedy and colour.
Raymond Mortimer, Sunday Times

Perceptive, lively, aware of the significance of trifles,
and a fine writer. Applied to a beautiful, various, and
still inscrutable country, these talents yield a
singularly delightful result.
The Times

This book has that ageless quality which is what
most people mean when they describe a book as
classical. From the moment that the train leaves
New York. . .it is certain that this journey will be
rewarding. When one finally leaves Mrs Bedford on
the point of departure, it is with the double regret of
leaving Mexico and her company, and one cannot
say more than that.
Elizabeth Jane Howard

Malicious, friendly, entertaining and witty.
Evening Standard

*If you wish to receive details of forthcoming publications,
please send your address to
Eland Books, 53 Eland Road, London SW11 5JX*

Previously published by
ELAND BOOKS

THE DEVIL DRIVES

A Life of Sir Richard Burton.

FAWN M. BRODIE

Richard Burton searched for the source of the Nile,
discovered Lake Tanganyika, and, at great risk,
penetrated the sacred cities of Medina and Mecca.
But he was much more than an explorer:
he was also an amateur botanist, swordsman,
zoologist and geologist. He wrote forty-three books,
translated erotica, and spoke forty languages and
dialects. His life is probably the most fascinating
and outlandish of all the Victorians.

A model of what a life of Burton should be.
Philip Toynbee, Observer

No one could fail to write a good life of Sir Richard
Burton (not even his wife), but Fawn Brodie has
written a brilliant one. Her scholarship is wide and
searching, and her understanding of Burton and
his wife both deep and wide. She writes with clarity
and zest. The result is a first class biography of an
exceptional man…Buy it, steal it, read it.
J. H. Plumb, New York Times

This edition is not for sale in the USA.

*If you wish to receive details of forthcoming publications,
please send your address to
Eland Books, 53 Eland Road, London SW11 5JX*

Previously published by
ELAND BOOKS

TRAVELS WITH MYSELF AND ANOTHER

MARTHA GELLHORN

Must surely be ranked as one of the funniest travel books of our time — second only to *A Short Walk in the Hindu Kush* . . . It doesn't matter whether this author is experiencing marrow-freezing misadventures in war-ravaged China, or driving a Landrover through East African game-parks, or conversing with hippies in Israel, or spending a week in a Moscow Intourist Hotel. Martha Gellhorn's reactions are what count and one enjoys equally her blistering scorn of humbug, her hilarious eccentricities, her unsentimental compassion.
Dervla Murphy, Irish Times

Spun with a fine blend of irony and epigram. She is incapable of writing a dull sentence.
The Times

Miss Gellhorn has a novelist's eye, a flair for black comedy and a short fuse . . . there is not a boring word in her humane and often funny book.
The New York Times

Among the funniest and best written books I have ever read.
Byron Rogers, Evening Standard

If you wish to receive details of forthcoming publications, please send your address to Eland Books, 53 Eland Road, London SW11 5JX

Previously published by

ELAND BOOKS

THE WEATHER IN AFRICA

MARTHA GELLHORN

This is a stunningly good book.
Victoria Glendinning, New York Times

She's a marvellous story-teller, and I think anyone who picks up this book is certainly not going to put it down again. One just wants to go on reading.
Francis King, Kaleidoscope, BBC Radio 4

An authentic sense of the divorce between Africa and what Europeans carry in their heads is powerfully conveyed by a prose that selects its details with care, yet remains cool in their expression.
Robert Nye, The Guardian

This is a pungent and witty book.
Jeremy Brooks, Sunday Times

If you wish to receive details of forthcoming publications,
please send your address to
Eland Books, 53 Eland Road, London SW11 5JX

A STATE OF FEAR

ANDREW GRAHAM-YOOLL
Memories of Argentina's nightmare

For ten hair-raising years Andrew Graham-Yooll
was the news editor for the Buenos Aires Herald.
All around him friends and acquaintances were
'disappearing'; and as an honest and brave
reporter he was under constant suspicion from all
sides in Argentina's war of fear.

Because of the author's obvious honesty and
level-headedness, we get an especially frightening
picture of life in a society where the slightest
deviation may cause you to disappear for ever.

'It is the story of trying to do two contradictory
things: write honestly and keep alive . . .
Gripping.'
Andrew Thompson, Guardian

'Will become a classic document about 20th
century Argentina . . . It is a small masterpiece.'
Hugh O'Shaugnessy, Financial Times

If you wish to receive details of forthcoming publications,
please send your address to
Eland Books, 53 Eland Road, London SW11 5JX

MOROCCO
THAT WAS

WALTER HARRIS

With a new preface by Patrick Thursfield

Both moving and hilariously satirical.
Gavin Maxwell, Lords of the Atlas

Many interesting sidelights on the customs and
characters of the Moors. . .intimate knowledge of
the courts, its language and customs. . .thorough
understanding of the Moorish character.
New York Times

No Englishman knows Morocco better than Mr W.
B. Harris and his new book. . .is most entertaining.
Spectator (1921)

The author's great love of Morocco and of the Moors
is only matched by his infectious zest for life. . .
thanks to his observant eye and a gift for felicitously
turned phrases, the books of Walter Harris can claim
to rank as literature.
Rom Landau, Moroccan Journal (1957)

His pages bring back the vanished days of the
unfettered Sultanate in all their dark splendour; a
mingling of magnificence with squalor, culture with
barbarism, refined cruelty with naive humour that
reads like a dream of the Arabian Nights.
The Times

*If you wish to receive details of forthcoming publications,
please send your address to
Eland Books, 53 Eland Road, London SW11 5JX*

Previously published by
ELAND BOOKS

HOLDING ON

A Novel by
MERVYN JONES

This is the story of a street in London's dockland
and of a family who lived in it. The street was built in
the 1880s, and the Wheelwright family (originally
dockers) lived there until its tragic demolition in
the 1960s, when it was replaced by tower blocks.
  As a social document, the book rings with truth,
but it is much more than that: its compelling
narrative brings the reader right into the life of the
Wheelright family and their neighbours.

Moving, intelligent, thoroughly readable…
it deserves a lot of readers.
Julian Symons, Sunday Times

A remarkable evocation of life in the East End of
London…Mr Jones fakes nothing and blurs little…
It is truthful and moving.
Guardian

Has a classic quality, for the reader feels
himself not an observer but a sharer in the life of
the Wheelwrights and their neighbours.
Daily Telegraph

*If you wish to receive details of forthcoming publications,
please send your address to
Eland Books, 53 Eland Road, London SW11 5JX*

THREE CAME HOME

AGNES KEITH
A woman's ordeal in a Japanese prison camp

Three Came Home should rank with the great imprisonment
stories of all times.
New York Herald Tribune

No one who reads her unforgettable narrative of the years she
passed in Borneo during the war years can fail to share her
emotions with something very like the intensity of a personal
experience.
Times Literary Supplement

This book sets a standard which will be difficult to surpass.
The Listener

It is one of the most remarkable books you will ever read.
John Carey, Sunday Times

*If you wish to receive details of forthcoming publications,
please send your address to
Eland Books, 53 Eland Road, London SW11 5JX*

A DRAGON APPARENT

NORMAN LEWIS
Travels in Cambodia, Laos and Vietnam

A book which should take its place in the permanent literature of the Far East.
Economist

One of the most absorbing travel books I have read for a very long time. . .the great charm of the work is its literary vividness. Nothing he describes is dull.
Peter Quennell, Daily Mail

One of the best post-war travel books and, in retrospect, the most heartrending.
The Observer

Apart from *The Quiet American*, which is of course a novel, the best book on Vietnam remains *A Dragon Apparent*.
Richard West, Spectator (1978)

One of the most elegant, witty, immensely readable, touching and tragic books I've ever read.
Edward Blishen, Radio 4

*If you wish to receive details of forthcoming publications,
please send your address to
Eland Books, 53 Eland Road, London SW11 5JX*

Previously published by

ELAND BOOKS

GOLDEN EARTH

NORMAN LEWIS

Travels in Burma

Mr Lewis can make even a lorry interesting.
Cyril Connolly, Sunday Times

Very funny . . . a really delightful book.
Maurice Collis, Observer

Norman Lewis remains the best travel writer alive.
Auberon Waugh, Business Traveller

The reader may find enormous pleasure here without knowing the country.
Honor Tracy, New Statesman

The brilliance of the Burmese scene is paralleled by the brilliance of the prose.
Guy Ramsey, Daily Telegraph

If you wish to receive details of forthcoming publications,
please send your address to
Eland Books, 53 Eland Road, London SW11 5JX

Previously published by
ELAND BOOKS

THE HONOURED SOCIETY

NORMAN LEWIS
The Sicilian Mafia Observed

New epilogue by Marcello Cimino

One of the great travel writers of our time.
Eric Newby, Observer

Mr Norman Lewis is one of the finest journalists
of his time. . .he excels both in finding material
and in evaluating it.
The Listener

It is deftly written, and every page is horribly
absorbing.
The Times

The Honoured Society is the most penetrating book
ever written on the Mafia.
Time Out

If you wish to receive details of forthcoming publications,
please send your address to
Eland Books, 53 Eland Road, London SW11 5JX

Previously published by

ELAND BOOKS

NAPLES '44

NORMAN LEWIS

As unique an experience for the reader as it must have been a unique experience for the writer.
Graham Greene

Uncommonly well written, entertaining despite its depressing content, and quite remarkably evocative.
Philip Toynbee, Observer

His ten novels and five non-fiction works place him in the front rank of contemporary English writers . . . here is a book of gripping fascination in its flow of bizarre anecdote and character sketch; and it is much more than that.
J. W. Lambert, Sunday Times

A wonderful book.
Richard West, Spectator

Sensitive, ironic and intelligent.
Paul Fussell, The New Republic

One goes on reading page after page as if eating cherries.
Luigi Barzini, New York Review of Books

This edition is not for sale in the USA

*If you wish to receive details of forthcoming publications,
please send your address to
Eland Books, 53 Eland Road, London SW11 5JX*

A VIEW
OF THE WORLD

NORMAN LEWIS
Selected Journalism

Here is the selected journalism of Norman Lewis, collected from a period of over thirty years. The selection includes ten of the best articles from *The Changing Sky*, eight more which have never been collected within a book, and two which have never previously been published.

From reviews of *The Changing Sky*:

He really goes in deep like a sharp polished knife. I have never travelled in my armchair so fast, variously and well.
V. S. Pritchett, New Statesman

He has compressed into these always entertaining and sophisticated sketches material that a duller man would have hoarded for half a dozen books.
The Times

Outstandingly the best travel writer of our age, if not the best since Marco Polo.
Auberon Waugh, Business Traveller

If you wish to receive details of forthcoming publications,
please send your address to
Eland Books, 53 Eland Road, London SW11 5JX

Previously published by
ELAND BOOKS

A YEAR IN
MARRAKESH

PETER MAYNE

A notable book, for the author is exceptional both in his literary talent and his outlook. His easy economical style seizes, with no sense of effort, the essence of people, situations and places ... Mr Mayne is that rare thing, a natural writer ... no less exceptional is his humour.
Few Westerners have written about Islam with so little nonsense and such understanding.
Times Literary Supplement.

He has contrived in a deceptively simple prose to disseminate in the air of an English November the spicy odours of North Africa; he has turned, for an hour, smog to shimmering sunlight. He has woven a texture of extraordinary charm.
Daily Telegraph

Mr Mayne's book gives us the 'strange elation' that good writing always creates. It is a good book, an interesting book, and one that I warmly recommend.
Harold Nicolson, Observer

*If you wish to receive details of forthcoming publications,
please send your address to
Eland Books, 53 Eland Road, London SW11 5JX*

Previously published by

ELAND BOOKS

KENYA DIARY (1902–1906)

RICHARD MEINERTZHAGEN

With a new preface by Elspeth Huxley

Those who have only read the tranquil descriptions of Kenya between the two Wars may be surprised by Meinertzhagen's often bloodthirsty diaries. They do not always make pleasant reading, but they offer an unrivalled and startlingly vivid account of life during the early days of the colony.

One of the best and most colourful intelligence officers the army ever had.
Times, Obituary

This book is of great interest and should not be missed
New Statesman

One of the ablest and most successful brains I had met in the army.
Lloyd George, Memoirs

Anybody at all interested in the evolution of Kenya or the workings of 'colonialism' would do well to read this diary.
William Plomer, Listener

If you wish to receive. details of forthcoming publications,
please send your address to
Eland Books, 53 Eland Road, London SW11 5JX

TRAVELS INTO THE INTERIOR OF AFRICA

MUNGO PARK

With a new preface by Jeremy Swift

Famous triumphs of exploration have rarely engendered outstanding books. *Travels into the Interior of Africa*, which has remained a classic since its first publication in 1799, is a remarkable exception.

It was a wonder that he survived so long, and a still greater one that his diaries could have been preserved . . . what amazing reading they make today!
Roy Kerridge, Tatler

The enthusiasm and understanding which informs Park's writing is irresistible.
Frances Dickenson, Time Out

One of the greatest and most respected explorers the world has known, a man of infinite courage and lofty principles, and one who dearly loved the black African.
E. W. Bovill, the Niger Explored

Told with a charm and naivety in themselves sufficient to captivate the most fastidious reader . . . modesty and truthfulness peep from every sentence . . . for actual hardships undergone, for dangers faced, and difficulties overcome, together with an exhibition of virtues which make a man great in the rude battle of life. Mungo Park stands without a rival.
Joseph Thomson, author of Through Masailand

*If you wish to receive details of forthcoming publications,
please send your address to
Eland Books, 53 Eland Road, London SW11 5JX*

Previously published by
ELAND BOOKS

LIGHTHOUSE
TONY PARKER

What is it that leads a man to make lighthouse-keeping his life's occupation? Why does he select a monotonous, lonely job which takes him away from his family for months at a stretch, leaving him in a cramped, narrow tower with two other men not of his own choosing?

Lighthouse-keepers and their families have opened their souls to Tony Parker, and his portrait of their lives is as compelling as any novel, and gives us an exceptional insight into the British character.

A very human book; and a pleasure to read.
John Fowles

Immediate, vivid, and absorbing... one of the most fascinating social documents I have ever read.
William Golding

A splendid book which has enriched my understanding of human nature.
Anthony Storr, The Sunday Times

If you wish to receive details of forthcoming publications,
please send your address to
Eland Books, 53 Eland Road, London SW11 5JX

A CURE FOR SERPENTS

THE DUKE OF PIRAJNO
An Italian doctor in North Africa

The Duke of Pirajno arrived in North Africa in 1924. For the next eighteen years, his experiences as a doctor in Libya, Eritrea, Ethiopia, and Somaliland provided him with opportunities and insights rarely given to a European. He brings us stories of noble chieftains and celebrated prostitutes, of Berber princes and Tuareg entertainers, of giant elephants and a lioness who fell in love with the author.

He tells us story after story with all the charm and resource of Scheherazade herself.
Harold Nicolson, Observer

A delightful personality, warm, observant, cynical and astringent. . .Doctors who are good raconteurs make wonderful reading.
Cyril Connolly, Sunday Times

A very good book indeed. . .He writes a rapid darting natural prose, like the jaunty scutter of a lizard on a rock.
Maurice Richardson, New Statesman

Pirajno's book is a cure for a great deal more than serpents.
The Guardian

In the class of book one wants to keep on a special shelf.
Doris Lessing, Good Book Guide

*If you wish to receive details of forthcoming publications,
please send your address to
Eland Books, 53 Eland Road, London SW11 5JX*

Previously published by
ELAND BOOKS

NUNAGA

DUNCAN PRYDE

Ten years among the Eskimos

Duncan Pryde, an eighteen-year-old orphan, an ex-merchant-seaman, and disgruntled factory worker left Glasgow for Canada to try his hand at fur-trading.

He became so absorbed in this new life that his next ten years were spent living with the Eskimos. He became part of their life even in its most intimate manifestations: hunting, shamanism, wife-exchange and blood feuds.

This record of these years is not only an astonishing adventure, but an unrivalled record of a way of life which, along with the igloo, has vanished altogether.

He tells us stories, which he seems to have been born to do.
Time

One of the best books about Arctic life ever written . . . A marvellous story, well told.
Sunday Times

*If you wish to receive details of forthcoming publications,
please send your address to
Eland Books, 53 Eland Road, London SW11 5JX*

Previously published by
ELAND BOOKS

A FUNNY OLD QUIST

The Memoirs of a Gamekeeper
EVAN ROGERS
EDITED BY CLIVE MURPHY

An octogenerian gamekeeper tells us his story.
He has worked for sixty-eight years on the same
Herefordshire estate, and can remember the time
when wooden clogs were worn and young women
gave birth in the fields while gathering stones for a
shilling a ton.

Although he is a downright traditionalist who
dislikes new-fangled ways, he doesn't pretend that
life was always easy, and he is sometimes sharply
critical of his former masters. From this truthful
and vivid account, we get an unsentimental picture
of life on a semi-feudal estate – a way of life that
has almost completely disappeared.

A refreshing and informative book, a social
document of permanent value, as well as a
good read.
Times Literary Supplement

Extraordinary is the proper word for it.
Country Life

*If you wish to receive details of forthcoming publications,
please send your address to
Eland Books, 53 Eland Road, London SW11 5JX*

Previously published by
ELAND BOOKS

THE LAW

A novel by
ROGER VAILLAND

With a new preface by Jonathan Keates

The Law is a cruel game that was played in the taverns of Southern Italy. It reflects the game of life in which the whole population of Manacore is engaged. Everyone from the feudal landowner, Don Cesare, to the landless day-labourers are participants in the never-ending contest.

Every paragraph and every section of this novel has been carefully cast and seems to be locked into position, creating a structure which is solid and formal, yet always lively. . .while we are reading the novel its world has an absolute validity. . . *The Law* is an experience I will not easily forget.
V. S. Naipaul, New Statesman

The Law deserves every reading it will have. It is and does all that a novel should – amuses, absorbs, excites and illuminates not only its chosen patch of ground but much more of life and character as well.
New York Times

One feels one knows everyone in the district. . .every page has the texture of living flesh.
New York Herald Tribune

A full rich book teeming with ambition, effort and desire as well as with ideas.
Times Literary Supplement

*If you wish to receive details of forthcoming publications,
please send your address to
Eland Books, 53 Eland Road, London SW11 5JX*